LOVE POEMS

SERIES EDITOR
DAVID STANFORD BURR

BARNES & NOBLE POETRY LIBRARY

Compilation copyright © 2002 by Barnes & Noble, Inc.
Foreword copyright © 2002 by David Stanford Burr

2002 Barnes & Noble Books

ISBN 0-7607-3311-2

Text design by Rhea Braunstein

Printed and bound in the United States of America

02 03 04 05 M 9 8 7 6 5 4 3 2

RRD-C

Contents

Foreword

Love Poems is an anthology of classic verse on affairs of the human heart in all its varieties reaching back over two-and-a-half millennia. From Ovid and Sappho in inspired translation to W. H. Auden and Elizabeth Bishop, many of the world's greatest poets originally, lyrically, and compellingly explore the rich emotion of love.

William Shakespeare compares his love to a summer's day. William Blake posits an answer to the important question "What is it men in women do require?" Elizabeth Barrett Browning counts the ways in "How do I love thee?" And Emily Dickinson reveals her hermit's passion in "Wild nights! Wild nights!" In the lines of these poems, lovers rejoice, the rejected suffer anguish (and sometimes plan revenge!), and the unrequited ache for that which will be denied to them forever. Here are poems of youthful "lust in action"; fond and distant reflections on a first love; laments for a spouse or lover who crossed over to the "silent land"; and musings on the loved one's clothes, accessories, or the innumerable attributes of her beauty or his handsomeness.

Christopher Smart amusingly apologizes to his lady for "being a little man"; Queen Elizabeth I poignantly regrets scorning those would-be wooers of her youth; and Walt Whitman "sings the body electric" in a sensuous sea of lovers and living and loving. Robert Burns, Lord Byron, E. E. Cummings, John Donne, Robert Frost, Thomas Hardy, John Keats, Edna St. Vincent Millay, Edgar Allan Poe, Christina Rossetti, Percy Bysshe Shelley, Lord Tennyson, Dylan Thomas, William Carlos Williams, and William Wordsworth, among many others, lend their voices to the common strain of love's enduring refrain.

As in Yeats's bittersweet "When You Are Old," I hope you will often "take down this book, / And slowly read, and dream the soft look / Your eyes had once" and soon may have again!

— DAVID STANFORD BURR

LOVE POEMS

"My lady carries love within her eyes;"

My lady carries love within her eyes;
　　All that she looks on is made pleasanter;
　　Upon her path men turn to gaze at her;
He whom she greeteth feels his heart to rise,
And droops his troubled visage, full of sighs,
　　And of his evil heart is then aware:
　　Hate loves, and pride becomes a worshipper.
O women, help to praise her in somewise.
Humbleness, and the hope that hopeth well,
　　By speech of hers into the mind are brought,
　　And who beholds is blessèd oftenwhiles.
　　The look she hath when she a little smiles
　　Cannot be said, nor holden in the thought;
'Tis such a new and gracious miracle.

Translated from the Italian by
Dante Gabriel Rossetti (1828–1882)

❧ The Wounded Cupid. Song

Cupid as he lay among
Roses, by a Bee was stung.
Whereupon in anger flying
To his Mother, said thus crying;
Help! O help! your Boy's a dying.
And why, my pretty Lad, said she?
Then blubbering, replied he,
A winged Snake has bitten me,
Which Country people call a Bee.
At which she smil'd; then with her hairs
And kisses drying up his tears:
Alas! said she, my Wag! if this
Such a pernicious torment is:
Come, tell me then, how great's the smart
Of those, thou woundest with thy Dart!

Translated from the Greek by
Robert Herrick (1591–1674)

ANACREON (570?–478? B.C.)

❧ Of Love, in honor of his Mistress Becchina

Whatever good is naturally done
   Is born of Love as fruit is born of flower:
   By Love all good is brought to its full power:
Yea, Love does more than this; for he finds none
So coarse but from his touch some grace is won,
   And the poor wretch is altered in an hour.
   So let it be decreed that Death devour
The beast who says that Love's a thing to shun.
A man's just worth the good that he can hold,
   And where no love is found, no good is there;
      On that there's nothing that I would not stake
So now, my Sonnet, go as you are told
   To lovers and their sweethearts everywhere,
      And say I made you for Becchina's sake.

Translated from the Italian by
Dante Gabriel Rossetti (1828–1882)

❧ A Lady laments for her lost Lover, by similitude of a Falcon

Alas for me, who loved a falcon well!
   So well I loved him, I was nearly dead:
   Ever at my low call he bent his head,
And ate of mine, not much, but all that fell.
Now he has fled, how high I cannot tell,
   Much higher now than ever he has fled,
   And is in a fair garden housed and fed;
Another lady, alas! shall love him well.
Oh, my own falcon whom I taught and rear'd!
   Sweet bells of shining gold I gave to thee
That in the chase though shouldst not be afeard.
   Now thou hast risen like the risen sea,
Broken thy jesses loose, and disappear'd,
   As soon as thou wast skilled in falconry.

Translated from the Italian by
Dante Gabriel Rossetti (1828–1882)

❧ Western Wind

Western wind, when will thou blow,
  The small rain down can rain?
Christ, if my love were in my arms
  And I in my bed again!

❧ "I saw my Lady weep,"

I saw my Lady weep,
And Sorrow proud to be advanced so
In those fair eyes, where all perfections keep;
    Her face was full of woe,
But such a woe (believe me) as wins more hearts
Than mirth can do, with her enticing parts.

Sorrow was there made fair,
And Passion, wise; Tears, a delightful thing;
Silence, beyond all speech, a wisdom rare;
    She made her sighs to sing,
And all things with so sweet a sadness move;
As made my heart both grieve and love.

O Fairer than aught else
The world can shew, leave off, in time, to grieve,
Enough, enough! Your joyful look excels;
    Tears kill the heart, believe,
O strive not to be excellent in woe,
Which only breeds your beauty's overthrow.

Fragment of a Song on the Beautiful Wife of Dr John Overall, Dean of St Paul's

The Dean of Paul's did search for his wife
    And where d'ee think he found her?
Even upon Sir John Selby's bed,
    As flat as any flounder.

There Is a Lady Sweet and Kind

There is a lady sweet and kind,
Was never face so pleased my mind;
I did but see her passing by,
And yet I love her till I die.

Her gesture, motion and her smiles,
Her wit, her voice, my heart beguiles,
Beguiles my heart, I know not why,
And yet I love her till I die.

Her free behavior, winning looks,
Will make a lawyer burn his books.
I touched her not, alas, not I,
And yet I love her till I die.

Had I her fast betwixt mine arms,
Judge you that think such sports were harms,
Were't any harm? No, no, fie, fie!
For I will love her till I die.

Should I remain confinèd there,
So long as Phoebus in his sphere,
I to request, she to deny,
Yet would I love her till I die.

ANONYMOUS (17TH CENTURY)

Cupid is wingèd and doth range;
Her country so my love doth change,
But change she earth, or change she sky,
Yet will I love her till I die.

❧ "I gently touched her hand: she gave"

I gently touched her hand: she gave
A look that did my soul enslave;
I pressed her rebel lips in vain:
They rose up to be pressed again.
  Thus happy, I no farther meant,
  Than to be pleased and innocent.

On her soft breasts my hand I laid,
And a quick, light impression made;
They with a kindly warmth did glow,
And swelled, and seemed to overflow.
  Yet, trust me, I no farther meant,
  Than to be pleased and innocent.

On her eyes my eyes did stay:
O'er her smooth limbs my hands did stray;
Each sense was ravished with delight,
And my soul stood prepared for flight.
  Blame me not if at last I meant
  More to be pleased than innocent.

The Coy Lass Dress'd Up in Her Best

Do not rumple my Top-Knot,
 I'll not be kiss'd to Day;
I'll not be hawled and pulled about,
 Thus on a Holy-day:
Then if your Rudeness you don't leave,
 No more is to be said:
See this long Pin upon my Sleeve,
 I'll run up to the Head;
And if you rumple my head Gear,
I'll give you a good flurt on the Ear.

Come upon a Worky-day,
 When I have my old Clothes on;
I shall not be so nice nor Coy,
 Nor stand so much upon:
Then hawl, and pull, and do your best,
 Yet I shall gentle be:
Kiss Hand, and Mouth, and fell my Breast,
 And tickle to my Knee:
I won't be put out of my rode,
You shall not rumple my Commode.

ANONYMOUS (18TH CENTURY)

❧ Bonny Barbara Allan

1

It was in and about the Martinmas time,
　When the green leaves were a falling,
That Sir John Græme, in the West Country,
　Fell in love with Barbara Allan.

2

He sent his man down through the town,
　To the place where she was dwelling:
"O haste and come to my master dear,
　Gin ye be Barbara Allan."

3

O hooly, hooly rose she up,
　To the place where he was lying,
And when she drew the curtain by:
　"Young man, I think you're dying."

4

"O it's I'm sick, and very, very sick,
　And 'tis a' for Barbara Allan."
"O the better for me ye s' never be,
　Though your heart's blood were a-spilling.

5

"O dinna ye mind, young man," said she,
　"When ye was in the tavern a drinking,
That ye made the healths gae round and round,
　And slighted Barbara Allan?"

6

He turned his face unto the wall,
　And death was with him dealing:
"Adieu, adieu, my dear friends all,
　And be kind to Barbara Allan."

7

And slowly, slowly raise she up,
　And slowly, slowly left him,
And sighing said, she could not stay,
　Since death of life had reft him.

8

She had not gane a mile but twa,
　When she heard the dead-bell ringing,
And every jow that the dead-bell geid,
　It cried, "Woe to Barbara Allan!"

9

"O mother, mother, make my bed!
　O make it saft and narrow!
Since my love died for me to-day,
　I'll die for him to-morrow."

ANONYMOUS (TRADITIONAL BALLAD)

❧ Lord Randal

1

"O where ha' you been, Lord Randal, my son?
And where ha' you been, my handsome young
  man?"
"I ha' been at the greenwood; mother, mak my
  bed soon,
For I'm wearied wi' huntin', and fain wad
  lie down."

2

"And wha met ye there, Lord Randal, my son?
And wha met you there, my handsome young
  man?"
"O I met wi' my true-love; mother, mak my
  bed soon,
For I'm wearied wi' huntin', and fain wad
  lie down."

3

"And what did she give you, Lord Randal, my son?
And what did she give you, my handsome young
  man?"
"Eels fried in a pan; mother, mak my bed soon,
For I'm wearied wi' huntin', and fain wad
  lie down."

ANONYMOUS (TRADITIONAL BALLAD)

"And wha gat your leavin's, Lord Randal, my son?
And wha gat your leavin's, my handsome young
   man?"
"My hawks and my hounds; mother, mak my
   bed soon,
For I'm wearied wi' huntin', and fain wad lie down."

5

"And what becam of them, Lord Randal, my son?
And what becam of them, my handsome young
   man?"
"They stretched their legs out and died; mother,
   mak my bed soon,
For I'm wearied wi' huntin', and fain wad lie down."

6

"O I fear you are poisoned, Lord Randal, my son!
I fear you are poisoned, my handsome young man!"
"Oh yes, I am poisoned; mother, mak my bed soon,
For I'm sick at the heart, and I fain wad lie down."

7

"What d' ye leave to your mother, Lord Randal,
   my son?
What d' ye leave to your mother, my handsome
   young man?"

stanza continues

ANONYMOUS (TRADITIONAL BALLAD)   15

"Four and twenty milk kye; mother, mak my bed
  soon,
For I'm sick at the heart, and I fain wad lie down."

8

"What d' ye leave to your sister, Lord Randal,
  my son?
What d' ye leave to your sister, my handsome
  young man?"
"My gold and my silver; mother, mak my bed soon,
For I'm sick at the heart, and I fain wad lie down."

9

"What d' ye leave to your brother, Lord Randal,
  my son?
What d' ye leave to your brother, my handsome
  young man?"
"My houses and my lands; mother, mak my bed
  soon,
For I'm sick at the heart, and I fain wad lie down."

10

"What d' ye leave to your true-love, Lord Randal,
  my son?
What d' ye leave to your true-love, my handsome
  young man?"
"I leave her hell and fire; mother, mak my bed soon,
For I'm sick at the heart, and I fain wad lie down."

✎ The Unquiet Grave

1

"The wind doth blow today, my love,
  And a few small drops of rain;
I never had but one true-love,
  In cold grave she was lain.

2

"I'll do as much for my true-love
  As any young man may;
I'll sit and mourn all at her grave
  For a twelvemonth and a day."

3

The twelvemonth and a day being up,
  The dead began to speak:
"Oh who sits weeping on my grave,
  And will not let me sleep?"

4

" 'T is I, my love, sits on your grave,
  And will not let you sleep;
For I crave one kiss of your clay-cold lips,
  And that is all I seek."

continues

ANONYMOUS (TRADITIONAL BALLAD)   17

5

"You crave one kiss of my clay-cold lips,
  But my breath smells earthy strong;
If you have one kiss from my clay-cold lips,
  Your time will not be long.

6

" 'T is down in yonder garden green,
  Love, where we used to walk,
The finest flower that e'er was seen
  Is withered to a stalk.

7

"The stalk is withered dry, my love,
  So will our hearts decay;
So make yourself content, my love,
  Till God calls you away."

❧ To Marguerite—Continued

Yes! in the sea of life enisled,
  With echoing straits between us thrown,
Dotting the shoreless watery wild,
  We mortal millions live *alone*.
The islands feel the enclasping flow,
And then their endless bounds they know.

But when the moon their hollows lights,
  And they are swept by balms of spring,
And in their glens, on starry nights,
  The nightingales divinely sing;
And lovely notes, from shore to shore,
Across the sounds and channels pour—

O! then a longing like despair
  Is to their farthest caverns sent;
For surely once, they feel, we were
  Parts of a single continent!
Now round us spreads the watery plain—
O might our marges meet again!

Who ordered that their longing's fire
  Should be, as soon as kindled, cooled?

stanza continues

MATTHEW ARNOLD (1822–1888)   19

Who renders vain their deep desire? —
  A God, a God their severance ruled!
And bade betwixt their shores to be
The unplumbed, salt, estranging sea.

❧ "Lay your sleeping head, my love,"

Lay your sleeping head, my love,
Human on my faithless arm;
Time and fevers burn away
Individual beauty from
Thoughtful children, and the grave
Proves the child ephemeral:
But in my arms till break of day
Let the living creature lie,
Mortal, guilty, but to me
The entirely beautiful.

Soul and body have no bounds:
To lovers as they lie upon
Her tolerant enchanted slope
In their ordinary swoon,
Grave the vision Venus sends
Of supernatural sympathy,
Universal love and hope;
While an abstract insight wakes
Among the glaciers and the rocks
The hermit's sensual ecstasy.

Certainty, fidelity
On the stroke of midnight pass

stanza continues

Like vibrations of a bell
And fashionable madmen raise
Their pedantic boring cry;
Every farthing of the cost,
All the dreaded cards foretell,
Shall be paid, but from this night
Not a whisper, not a thought,
Not a kiss nor look be lost.

Beauty, midnight, vision dies:
Let the winds of dawn that blow
Softly round your dreaming head
Such a day of sweetness show
Eye and knocking heart may bless,
Find the mortal world enough;
Noons of dryness see you fed
By the involuntary powers,
Nights of insult let you pass
Watched by every human love.

W. H. AUDEN (1907–1973)

❧ Insomnia

The moon in the bureau mirror
looks out a million miles
(and perhaps with pride, at herself,
but she never, never smiles)
far and away beyond sleep, or
perhaps she's a daytime sleeper.

By the Universe deserted,
she'd tell it to go to hell,
and she'd find a body of water,
or a mirror, on which to dwell.
So wrap up care in a cobweb
and drop it down the well

into that world inverted
where left is always right,
where the shadows are really the body,
where we stay awake all night,
where the heavens are shallow as the sea
is now deep, and you love me.

❧ A Question Answered

What is it men in women do require?
The lineaments of Gratified Desire.
What is it women do in men require?
The lineaments of Gratified Desire.

❧ My Pretty Rose-Tree

A flower was offered to me,
Such a flower as May never bore;
But I said 'I've a Pretty Rose-tree,'
And I passed the sweet flower o'er.

Then I went to my Pretty Rose-tree,
To tend her by day and by night;
But my Rose turned away with jealousy,
And her thorns were my only delight.

The Garden of Love

I went to the Garden of Love,
And saw what I never had seen:
A Chapel was built in the midst,
Where I used to play on the green.

And the gates of this Chapel were shut,
And "Thou shalt not" writ over the door;
So I turn'd to the Garden of Love,
That so many sweet flowers bore,

And I saw it was filled with graves,
And tomb-stones where flowers should be:
And Priests in black gowns were walking their
    rounds,
And binding with briars my joys & desires.

❧ The Smile

There is a smile of love,
And there is a smile of deceit,
And there is a smile of smiles
In which these two smiles meet.

And there is a frown of hate,
And there is a frown of disdain,
And there is a frown of frowns
Which you strive to forget in vain.

For it sticks in the heart's deep core,
And it sticks in the deep backbone.
And no Smile that ever was smiled
But only one smile alone,

And betwixt the cradle and grave
It only once smiled can be;
But when it once is smiled,
There's an end to all misery.

❧ Farewell to Juliet

I see you, Juliet, still, with your straw hat
Loaded with vines, and with your dear pale face,
On which those thirty years so lightly sat,
And the white outline of your muslin dress.
You wore a little *fichu* trimmed with lace
And crossed in front, as was the fashion then,
Bound at your waist with a broad band or sash,
All white and fresh and virginally plain.
There was a sound of shouting far away
Down in the valley, as they called to us,
And you, with hands clasped seeming still to pray
Patience of fate, stood listening to me thus
With heaving bosom. There a rose lay curled.
It was the reddest rose in all the world.

　　　　　　WILFRID BLUNT (1840–1922)

"The night has a thousand eyes,"

The night has a thousand eyes,
  And the day but one;
Yet the light of the bright world dies
  With the dying sun.

The mind has a thousand eyes,
  And the heart but one;
Yet the light of a whole life dies
  When love is done.

FRANCIS WILLIAM BOURDILLON (1852–1921) 29

❧ A Letter to Her Husband, Absent upon Public Employment

My head, my heart, mine eyes, my life, nay, more,
My joy, my magazine of earthly store,
If two be one, as surely thou and I,
How stayest thou there, whilst I at Ipswich lie?
So many steps, head from the heart to sever,
If but a neck, soon should we be together.
I, like the Earth this season, mourn in black,
My Sun is gone so far in's zodiac,
Whom whilst I 'joyed, nor storms, nor frost I felt,
His warmth such frigid colds did cause to melt.
My chillèd limbs now numbèd lie forlorn;
Return; return, sweet Sol, from Capricorn;
In this dead time, alas, what can I more
Than view those fruits which through thy heat I bore?
Which sweet contentment yield me for a space,
True living pictures of their father's face.
O strange effect! now thou art southward gone,
I weary grow the tedious day so long;
But when thou northward to me shalt return,
I wish my Sun may never set, but burn
Within the Cancer of my glowing breast,
The welcome house of him my dearest guest.

Where ever, ever stay, and go not thence,
Till nature's sad decree shall call thee hence;
Flesh of thy flesh, bone of thy bone,
I here, thou there, yet both but one.

❧ Remembrance

Cold in the earth—and the deep snow piled
   above thee,
Far, far removed, cold in the dreary grave!
Have I forgot, my only Love, to love thee,
Severed at last by Time's all-severing wave?

Now, when alone, do my thoughts no longer hover
Over the mountains, on that northern shore,
Resting their wings where heath and fern leaves
   cover
Thy noble heart forever, ever more?

Cold in the earth—and fifteen wild Decembers,
From those brown hills, have melted into spring;
Faithful, indeed, is the spirit that remembers
After such years of change and suffering!

Sweet Love of youth, forgive, if I forget thee,
While the world's tide is bearing me along;
Other desires and other hopes beset me,
Hopes which obscure, but cannot do thee wrong!

No later light has lightened up my heaven,
No second morn has ever shone for me;

stanza continues

EMILY BRONTË (1818–1848)

All my life's bliss from thy dear life was given,
All my life's bliss is in the grave with thee.

But, when the days of golden dreams had perished,
And even Despair was powerless to destroy,
Then did I learn how existence could be cherished,
Strengthened, and fed without the aid of joy.

Then did I check the tears of useless passion —
Weaned my young soul from yearning after thine;
Sternly denied its burning wish to hasten
Down to that tomb already more than mine.

And, even yet, I dare not let it languish,
Dare not indulge in memory's rapturous pain;
Once drinking deep of that divinest anguish,
How could I seek the empty world again?

❧ The Hill

Breathless we flung us on the windy hill,
  Laughed in the sun, and kissed the lovely grass.
  You said, "Through glory and ecstasy we pass;
Wind, sun, and earth remain, the birds sing still,
When we are old, are old. . . ." "And when we die
  All's over that is ours; and life burns on
Through other lovers, other lips," said I,
  —"Heart of my heart, our heaven is now,
    is won!"

"We are Earth's best, that learnt her lesson here.
  Life is our cry. We have kept the faith!" we said;
  "We shall go down with unreluctant tread
Rose-crowned into the darkness!" . . . Proud
    we were,
  And laughed, that had such brave true things
    to say.
  —And then you suddenly cried, and turned
    away.

RUPERT BROOKE (1887–1915)

 # Sonnet XIV

from *SONNETS FROM THE PORTUGUESE*

If thou must love me, let it be for naught
Except for love's sake only. Do not say,
"I love her for her smile—her look—her way
Of speaking gently—for a trick of thought
That falls in well with mine, and certes brought
A sense of pleasant ease on such a day"—
For these things in themselves, Belovèd, may
Be changed, or change for thee—and love, so
   wrought,
May be unwrought so. Neither love me for
Thine own dear pity's wiping my cheeks dry:
A creature might forget to weep, who bore
Thy comfort long, and lose thy love thereby!
But love me for love's sake, that evermore
Thou may'st love on, through love's eternity.

❧ Sonnet XLIII

from *SONNETS FROM THE PORTUGUESE*

How do I love thee? Let me count the ways.
I love thee to the depth and breadth and height
My soul can reach, when feeling out of sight
For the ends of Being and ideal Grace.
I love thee to the level of every day's
Most quiet need, by sun and candlelight.
I love thee freely, as men strive for Right;
I love thee purely, as they turn from Praise.
I love thee with the passion put to use
In my old griefs, and with my childhood's faith.
I love thee with a love I seemed to lose
With my lost saints,—I love thee with the breath,
Smiles, tears, of all my life!—and, if God choose,
I shall but love thee better after death.

A Woman's Last Word

Let's contend no more, Love,
  Strive nor weep;
All be as before, Love,
  —Only sleep!

What so wild as words are?
  I and thou
In debate, as birds are,
  Hawk on bough!

See the creature stalking
  While we speak!
Hush and hide the talking,
  Cheek on cheek!

What so fast as truth is,
  False to thee?
Where the serpent's tooth is
  Shun the tree—

Where the apple reddens
  Never pry—
Lest we lose our Edens,
  Eve and I.

continues

ROBERT BROWNING (1812–1889)   37

Be a god and hold me
  With a charm!
Be a man and fold me
  With thine arm!

Teach me, only teach, Love!
  As I ought
I will speak thy speech, Love,
  Think thy thought —

Meet, if thou require it,
  Both demands,
Laying flesh and spirit
  In thy hands.

That shall be tomorrow
  Not tonight:
I must bury sorrow
  Out of sight:

— Must a little weep, Love,
  (Foolish me!)
And so fall asleep, Love,
  Loved by thee.

Meeting at Night

The grey sea and the long black land;
And the yellow half-moon large and low;
And the startled little waves that leap
In fiery ringlets from their sleep,
As I gain the cove with pushing prow,
And quench its speed in the slushy sand.

Then a mile of warm sea-scented beach;
Three fields to cross till a farm appears;
A tap at the pane, the quick sharp scratch
And blue spurt of a lighted match,
And a voice less loud, thro' its joys and fears,
Than the two hearts beating each to each!

The Lost Mistress

All's over, then: does truth sound bitter
   As one at first believes?
Hark, 'tis the sparrows' good-night twitter
   About your cottage eaves!

And the leaf-buds on the vine are woolly,
   I noticed that, today;
One day more bursts them open fully
   —You know the red turns grey.

Tomorrow we meet the same then, dearest?
   May I take your hand in mine?
Mere friends are we,—well, friends the merest
   Keep much that I resign:

For each glance of the eye so bright and black,
   Though I keep with heart's endeavour,—
Your voice, when you wish the snowdrops back,
   Though it stay in my soul for ever!—

Yet I will but say what mere friends say,
   Or only a thought stronger;
I will hold your hand but as long as all may,
   Or so very little longer!

ROBERT BROWNING (1812–1889)

A Red Red Rose

O my Luve's like a red, red rose,
  That's newly sprung in June;
O my Luve's like the melodie
  That's sweetly play'd in tune.—

As fair art thou, my bonie lass,
  So deep in luve am I;
And I will love thee still, my Dear,
  Till a' the seas gang dry.—

Till a' the seas gang dry, my Dear,
  And the rocks melt wi' the sun:
I will love thee still, my Dear,
  While the sands o' life shall run.—

And fare thee weel, my only Luve!
  And fare thee weel, a while!
And I will come again, my Luve,
  Tho' it were ten thousand mile!

❧ Bonie Doon

Ye flowery banks o' bonie Doon,
    How can ye blume sae fair?
How can ye chant, ye little birds,
    And I sae fu' o' care?

Thou'll break my heart, thou bonie bird,
    That sings upon the bough;
Thou minds me o' the happy days,
    When my fause luve was true.

Thou'll break my heart, thou bonie bird,
    That sings beside thy mate;
For sae I sat, and sae I sang,
    And wist na o' my fate.

Aft hae I roved by bonie Doon
    To see the wood-bine twine,
And ilka bird sang o' its luve,
    And sae did I o' mine.

Wi' lightsome heart I pu'd a rose
    Frae aff its thorny tree;
And my fause luver staw my rose
    But left the thorn wi' me.

John Anderson, My Jo

John Anderson my jo, John,
  When we were first acquent,
Your locks were like the raven,
  Your bonie brow was brent;
But now your brow is beld, John,
  Your locks are like the snow;
But blessings on your frost pow,
  John Anderson, my jo.

John Anderson my jo, John,
  We clamb the hill thegither;
And mony a canty day, John,
  We've had wi' ane anither:
Now we maun totter down, John,
  And hand in hand we'll go,
And sleep thegither at the foot,
  John Anderson, my jo.

❧ Coming

. . . for Joan

Tonight I walk the dirt road's crown to you
through fat fairy snowflakes falling down, each
a white paper lantern glowing the way.
It will be an hour more till I nose
the wood smoke from our cabin in the woods
that resiny scent I could follow blind.

It's so still even with the muffled crunch
of my footfalls and the plumes of breath pants
and the blood throb in my ears and the faint
crackle nearby flakes make as they touch down.
I smell your fire and grow warm, but I'm not
home yet—another twenty minutes more.

Now there's the slight flicker in the saplings
your candle gutters in the front window.
I stamp the stoop, open the door, enter
and in a rush you are all over me
dusting off the snow, pulling my coat off,
melting me with that smile I came for.

DAVID STANFORD BURR (B. 1955)

❧ She Walks in Beauty

She walks in beauty, like the night
   Of cloudless climes and starry skies;
And all that's best of dark and bright
   Meet in her aspect and her eyes:
Thus mellowed to that tender light
   Which heaven to gaudy day denies.

One shade the more, one ray the less,
   Had half impaired the nameless grace
Which waves in every raven tress,
   Or softly lightens o'er her face;
Where thoughts serenely sweet express
   How pure, how dear their dwelling place.

And on that cheek, and o'er that brow,
   So soft, so calm, yet eloquent,
The smiles that win, the tints that glow,
   But tell of days in goodness spent,
A mind at peace with all below,
   A heart whose love is innocent!

So We'll Go No More A-Roving

1

So we'll go no more a-roving
   So late into the night,
Though the heart be still as loving,
   And the moon be still as bright.

2

For the sword outwears its sheath,
   And the soul wears out the breast,
And the heart must pause to breathe,
   And love itself have rest.

3

Though the night was made for loving,
   And the day returns too soon,
Yet we'll go no more a-roving
   By the light of the moon.

　　　　　　　LORD BYRON (1788–1824)

When We Two Parted

When we two parted
　　In silence and tears,
Half broken-hearted
　　To sever for years,
Pale grew thy cheek and cold,
　　Colder thy kiss;
Truly that hour foretold
　　Sorrow to this.

The dew of the morning
　　Sunk chill on my brow—
It felt like the warning
　　Of what I feel now.
Thy vows are all broken,
　　And light is thy fame;
I hear thy name spoken,
　　And share in its shame.

They name thee before me,
　　A knell to mine ear;
A shudder comes o'er me—
　　Why wert thou so dear?

stanza continues

They know not I knew thee,
  Who knew thee too well—
Long, long shall I rue thee,
  Too deeply to tell.

In secret we met—
  In silence I grieve,
That thy heart could forget,
  Thy spirit deceive.
If I should meet thee
  After long years,
How should I greet thee?—
  With silence and tears.

LORD BYRON (1788–1824)

❧ My Sweetest Lesbia

My sweetest Lesbia, let us live and love,
And though the sager sort our deeds reprove,
Let us not weigh them. Heaven's great lamps
   do dive
Into their west, and straight again revive,
But soon as once set is our little light,
Then must we sleep one ever-during night.

If all would lead their lives in love like me,
Then bloody swords and armor should not be;
No drum nor trumpet peaceful sleeps should move,
Unless alarm came from the camp of love.
But fools do live, and waste their little light,
And seek with pain their ever-during night.

When timely death my life and fortune ends,
Let not my hearse be vexed with mourning friends,
But let all lovers, rich in triumph, come
And with sweet pastimes grace my happy tomb;
And Lesbia, close up thou my little light,
And crown with love my ever-during night.

THOMAS CAMPION (1567–1620)
49

Vobiscum Est Iope

When thou must home to shades of underground,
And there arrived, a new admirèd guest,
The beauteous spirits do engirt thee round,
White Iope, blithe Helen, and the rest,
To hear the stories of thy finished love
From that smooth tongue whose music hell
  can move;

Then wilt thou speak of banqueting delights,
Of masques and revels which sweet youth
  did make,
Of tourneys and great challenges of knights,
And all these triumphs for thy beauty's sake:
When thou hast told these honours done to thee,
Then tell, O tell, how thou didst murder me!

On the Marriage of T.K. and C.C., the Morning Stormy

Such should this day be, so the sun should hide
His bashful face, and let the conquering Bride
Without a rival shine, whilst he forbears
To mingle his unequal beams with hers;
Or if sometimes he glance his squinting eye
Between the parting clouds, 'tis but to spy,
Not emulate her glories, so comes dressed
In veils, but as a masquer to the feast.
Thus heaven should lower, such stormy gusts
   should blow
Not to denounce ungentle Fates, but show
The cheerful Bridegroom to the clouds and wind
Hath all his tears, and all his sighs assigned.
Let tempests struggle in the air, but rest
Eternal calms within thy peaceful breast,
Thrice happy Youth; but ever sacrifice
To that fair hand that dried thy blubbered eyes,
That crowned thy head with roses, and turned all
The plagues of love into a cordial,
When first it joined her virgin snow to thine,
Which when today the Priest shall recombine,

continues

From the mysterious holy touch such charms
Will flow, as shall unlock her wreathèd arms,
And open a free passage to that fruit
Which thou hast toiled for with a long pursuit.
But ere thou feed, that thou may'st better taste
Thy present joys, think on thy torments past.
Think on the mercy freed thee, think upon
Her virtues, graces, beauties, one by one,
So shalt thou relish all, enjoy the whole
Delights of her fair body, and pure soul.
Then boldly to the fight of love proceed,
'Tis mercy not to pity though she bleed,
We'll strew no nuts, but change that ancient form,
For till tomorrow we'll prorogue this storm,
Which shall confound with its loud whistling noise
Her pleasing shrieks, and fan thy panting joys.

Secrecy Protested

Fear not (dear Love) that I'll reveal
Those hours of pleasure we two steal;
No eye shall see, nor yet the Sun
Descry what thou and I have done;

No ear shall hear our love, but we
Silent as the night will be;
The god of love himself (whose dart
Did first wound mine and then thy heart),

Shall never know, that we can tell,
What sweets in stol'n embraces dwell.
This only meanes may find it out,
If, when I die, physicians doubt

What caus'd my death, and there to view
Of all their judgments which was true —
Rip up my heart, oh! then, I fear,
The world will see thy picture there.

❧ To My Inconstant Mistress

When thou, poor excommunicate
   From all the joys of love, shalt see
The full reward and glorious fate
   Which my strong faith shall purchase me,
   Then curse thine own inconstancy.

A fairer hand than thine shall cure
   That heart which thy false oaths did wound,
And to my soul a soul more pure
   Than thine shall by Love's hand be bound,
   And both with equal glory crowned.

Then shalt thou weep, entreat, complain
   To Love, as I did once to thee;
When all thy tears shall be as vain
   As mine were then, for thou shalt be
   Damned for thy false apostasy.

THOMAS CAREW (1594?–1640)

❧ Song of Troilus

from *TROILUS AND CRISEYDE*

"If no love is, O God, what fele I so?
And if love is, what thing and whiche is he!
If love be good, from whennes comth my wo?
If it be wikke, a wonder thinketh me,
Whenne every torment and adversitee
That cometh of hym, may to me savory thinke;
For ay thurst I, the more that I it drinke.

And if that at myn owen lust I brenne,
From whennes cometh my wailing and my pleynte?
If harm agree me, where-to pleyne I thenne?
I noot ne why unwery that I feynte.
O quike deth, O swete harm so queynte,
How may of thee in me swich quantitee,
But if that I consente that it be?

And if that I consente, I wrongfully
Compleyne, y-wis; thus possed to and fro,
Al sterelees with-inne a boat am I
A-mid the see, by twixen windes two
That in contrarie stonden ever-mo.
Allas! what is this wonder maladye?
For hete or cold, for cold of hete, I deye."

❧ First Love

I ne'er was struck before that hour
  With love so sudden and so sweet,
Her face it bloomed like a sweet flower
  And stole my heart away complete.
My face turned pale as deadly pale.
  My legs refused to walk away,
And when she looked, what could I ail?
  My life and all seemed turned to clay.

And then my blood rushed to my face
  And took my eyesight quite away.
The trees and bushes round the place
  Seemed midnight at noonday.
I could not see a single thing,
  Words from my eyes did start—
They spoke as chords do from the string,
  And blood burnt round my heart.

Are flowers the winter's choice?
  Is love's bed always snow?
She seemed to hear my silent voice,
  Not love's appeals to know.
I never saw so sweet a face
  As that I stood before.
My heart has left its dwelling-place
  And can return no more.

JOHN CLARE (1793–1864)

"My True Love Hath My Heart and I Have His"

None ever was in love with me but grief.
  She wooed me from the day that I was born;
She stole my playthings first, the jealous thief,
  And left me there forlorn.

The birds that in my garden would have sung,
  She scared away with her unending moan;
She slew my lovers too when I was young,
  And left me there alone.

Grief, I have cursed thee often—now at last
  To hate thy name I am no longer free;
Caught in thy bony arms and prisoned fast,
  I love no love but thee.

(Note: This poem's title derives from Sir Philip Sidney's "My true love hath my heart, and I have his.")

"False though she be to me and love,"

False though she be to me and love,
    I'll ne'er pursue revenge;
For still the charmer I approve,
    Though I deplore her change.

In hours of bliss we oft have met;
    They could not always last:
And though the present I regret,
    I'm grateful for the past.

~ "i like my body when it is with your"

i like my body when it is with your
body.   It is so quite new a thing.
Muscles better and nerves more.
i like your body.   i like what it does,
i like its hows.   i like to feel the spine
of your body and its bones,and the trembling
-firm-smooth ness and which i will
again and again and again
kiss,   i like kissing this and that of you,
i like,slowly stroking the,shocking fuzz
of your electric fur,and what-is-it comes
over parting flesh....And eyes big love-crumbs,

and possibly i like the thrill

of under me you so quite new

❧ "If you would know the reason why"

If you would know the reason why
   But half a song I bring,
I have—alas, I must reply—
   But half a theme to sing!
'Tis I alone that feel the spell;
   'Tis I alone that burn:
The lady that I love so well
   My love will not return.

I'll take the "No" she deigns to give,
   Since she withholds the "Yes;"
Better with her in hope to live
   Than elsewhere to possess!
Since with my fate I cannot cope,
   Shall this my solace prove—
To dream that she, as whispers hope,
   May one day learn to love.

Translated from the Provençal by
John Rutherford (19th century)

❧ The Smiling Mouth

The smiling mouth and laughing eyen gray,
The breastes round and long small armes twain,
   The handes smooth, the sides straight and plain,
Your feetes lit—what should I further say?
It is my craft when ye are far away
   To muse thereon in stinting of my pain—
The smiling mouth and laughing eyen gray,
   The breastes round and long small armes twain.
So would I pray you, if I durst or may,
   The sight to see as I have seen,
   Forwhy that craft me is most fain,
And will be to the hour in which I day—
The smiling mouth and laughing eyen gray,
   The breastes round and long small armes twain.

❧ *from* "When sere leaf falleth"

Of love's wayfaring
   I know no part to blame,
All other paring,
   compared, is put to shame,
Man can acclaim
   no second for comparing
With her, no dame
   but hath the meaner bearing.

I'ld ne'er entangle
   my heart with other fere,
Although I mangle
   my joy by staying here
I have no fear
   that ever at Pontrangle
You'll find her peer
   or one that's worth a wrangle.

She'd ne'er destroy
   her man with cruelty
'Twixt here 'n' Savoy
   there feeds no fairer she,
Than pleaseth me
   till Paris had ne'er joy
In such degree
   from Helena in Troy.

She's so the rarest
    who holdeth me thus gay,
The thirty fairest
    can not contest her sway;
'Tis right, par fay,
    thou know. O song that wearest
Such bright array,
    whose quality thou sharest. . . .

Translated from the Provençal by
Ezra Pound (1885–1972)

❧ "I cannot live with you,"

I cannot live with you,
It would be life,
And life is over there
Behind the shelf

The sexton keeps the key to,
Putting up
Our life, his porcelain,
Like a cup

Discarded of the housewife,
Quaint or broken;
A newer Sèvres pleases,
Old ones crack.

I could not die with you,
For one must wait
To shut the other's gaze down,—
You could not.

And I, could I stand by
And see you freeze,
Without my right of frost,
Death's privilege?

Nor could I rise with you,
Because your face
Would put out Jesus',
That new grace

Glow plain and foreign
On my homesick eye,
Except that you, than he
Shone closer by.

They'd judge us—how?
For you served Heaven, you know,
Or sought to;
I could not,

Because you saturated sight,
And I had no more eyes
For sordid excellence
As Paradise.

And were you lost, I would be,
Though my name
Rang loudest
On the heavenly fame.

continues

EMILY DICKINSON (1830–1886)　　　　65

And were you saved,
And I condemned to be
Where you were not,
That self were hell to me.

So we must keep apart,
You there, I here,
With just the door ajar
That oceans are,
And prayer,
And that pale sustenance,
Despair!

❧ "My life closed twice before its close;"

My life closed twice before its close;
   It yet remains to see
If Immortality unveil
   A third event to me,

So huge, so hopeless to conceive,
   As these that twice befell.
Parting is all we know of heaven,
   And all we need of hell.

❧ "Wild nights! Wild nights!"

Wild nights! Wild nights!
Were I with thee,
Wild nights should be
Our luxury!

Futile the winds
To a heart in port, —
Done with the compass,
Done with the chart.

Rowing in Eden!
Ah! the sea!
Might I but moor
To-night in thee!

A Valediction Forbidding Mourning

As virtuous men pass mildly' away,
  And whisper to their souls to go,
Whilst some of their sad friends do say
  The breath goes now, and some say, no;

So let us melt, and make no noise,
  No tear-floods, nor sigh-tempests move,
'Twere profanation of our joys
  To tell the laity our love.

Moving of th' earth brings harms and fears,
  Men reckon what it did and meant;
But trepidation of the spheres,
  Though greater far, is innocent.

Dull sublunary lovers' love
  (Whose soul is sense) cannot admit
Absence, because it doth remove
  Those things which elemented it.

But we by' a love so much refined
  That our selves know not what it is,
Inter-assurèd of the mind,
  Care less, eyes, lips, and hands to miss.

continues

JOHN DONNE (1572–1631)

Our two souls therefore, which are one,
  Though I must go, endure not yet
A breach, but an expansion,
  Like gold to airy thinness beat.

If they be two, they are two so
  As stiff twin compasses are two;
Thy soul, the fixed foot, makes no show
  To move, but doth, if th' other do.

And though it in the center sit,
  Yet when the other far doth roam,
It leans and hearkens after it,
  And grows erect, as that comes home.

Such wilt thou be to me, who must
  Like th' other foot, obliquely run.
Thy firmness makes my circle just,
  And makes me end where I begun.

❧ Break of Day

Stay, O sweet, and do not rise
The light that shines comes from thine eyes;
The day breaks not, it is my heart,
Because that you and I must part.
　　Stay, or else my joys will die,
　　And perish in their infancy.

'Tis true 'tis day; what though it be?
O, wilt thou therefore rise from me?
Why should we rise because 'tis light?
Did we lie down because 'twas night?
Love which in spite of darkness brought us hither,
Should in despite of light keep us together.

Light hath no tongue, but is all eye;
If it could speak as well as spy,
This were the worst that it could say,
That being well I fain would stay,
And that I lov'd my heart and honour so,
That I would not from him that had them go.

Must business thee from hence remove?
O that's the worst disease of love;

stanza continues

JOHN DONNE (1572–1631)

The poor, the foul, the false, love can
Admit, but not the busied man.
He which hath business, and makes love, doth do
Such wrong, as when a married man doth woo.

〜 "Sweetest love, I do not go"

Sweetest love, I do not go
  For weariness of thee,
Nor in hope the world can show
  A fitter love for me;
    But since that I
Must die at last, 'tis best
To use myself in jest,
  Thus by feigned deaths to die.

Yesternight the sun went hence,
  And yet is here today;
He hath no desire nor sense,
  Nor half so short a way:
    Then fear not me,
But believe that I shall make
Speedier journeys, since I take
  More wings and spurs than he.

O how feeble is man's power,
  That if good fortune fall,
Cannot add another hour,
  Nor a lost hour recall!

stanza continues

But come bad chance,
And we join to'it our strength,
And we teach it art and length,
    Itself o'er us to'advance.

When thou sigh'st, thou sigh'st not wind,
    But sigh'st my soul away;
When thou weep'st, unkindly kind,
    My life's blood doth decay.
        It cannot be
That thou lov'st me, as thou say'st,
If in thine my life thou waste;
    Thou art the best of me.

Let not thy divining heart
    Forethink me any ill;
Destiny may take thy part,
    And may thy fears fulfill;
        But think that we
Are but turned aside to sleep;
They who one another keep
    Alive, ne'er parted be.

∾ The Expiration

So, so, break off this last lamenting kiss,
   Which sucks two souls, and vapours Both away,
Turn thou ghost that way, and let me turn this,
   And let our selves benight our happiest day,
We ask'd none leave to love; nor will we owe
   Any, so cheap a death, as saying, Go;

Go; and if that word have not quite kill'd thee,
   Ease me with death, by bidding me go too.
Oh, if it have, let my word work on me,
   And a just office on a murderer do.
Except it be too late, to kill me so,
   Being double dead, going, and bidding, go.

❧ The Flea

Mark but this flea, and mark in this,
How little that which thou deny'st me is;
  Me it sucked first, and now sucks thee,
And in this flea, our two bloods mingled be;
  Confess it, this cannot be said
A sin, or shame, or loss of maidenhead,
    Yet this enjoys before it woo,
And pampered swells with one blood made of two,
And this, alas, is more than we would do.

Oh stay, three lives in one flea spare,
Where we almost, nay more than married are:
  This flea is you and I, and this
Our marriage bed, and marriage temple is;
  Though parents grudge, and you, we're met,
And cloistered in these living walls of jet.
    Though use make thee apt to kill me,
Let not to this, self murder added be,
And sacrilege, three sins in killing three.

Cruel and sudden, hast thou since
Purpled thy nail, in blood of innocence?
  In what could this flea guilty be,
Except in that drop which it sucked from thee?

stanza continues

Yet thou triumph'st, and say'st that thou
Find'st not thyself, nor me the weaker now;
   'Tis true, then learn how false, fears be;
Just so much honour, when thou yield'st to me,
Will waste, as this flea's death took life from thee.

The Good-Morrow

I wonder, by my troth, what thou and I
Did, till we loved? were we not weaned till then?
But sucked on country pleasures, childishly?
Or snorted we in the Seven Sleepers' den?
'Twas so; but this, all pleasures fancies be.
If ever any beauty I did see,
Which I desired, and got, 'twas but a dream
   of thee.

And now good-morrow to our waking souls,
Which watch not one another out of fear;
For love, all love of other sights controls,
And makes one little room an everywhere.
Let sea-discoverers to new worlds have gone,
Let maps to others, worlds on worlds have shown,
Let us possess one world, each hath one, and
   is one.

My face in thine eye, thine in mine appears,
And true plain hearts do in the faces rest;
Where can we find two better hemispheres,
Without sharp North, without declining West?
Whatever dies was not mixed equally;
If our two loves be one, or, thou and I
Love so alike that none do slacken, none can die.

                                    JOHN DONNE (1572–1631)

❧ The Sun Rising

Busy old fool, unruly Sun,
   Why dost thou thus,
Through windows, and through curtains call
  on us?
Must to thy motions lovers' seasons run?
    Saucy pedantic wretch, go chide
    Late school-boys, and sour 'prentices,
   Go tell court-huntsmen that the King will ride,
   Call country ants to harvest offices;
Love, all alike, no season knows, nor clime,
Nor hours, days, months, which are the rags
  of time.

Thy beams, so reverend, and strong
   Why shouldst thou think?
I could eclipse and cloud them with a wink,
But that I would not lose her sight so long:
    If her eyes have not blinded thine,
    Look, and tomorrow late, tell me,
   Whether both the Indias of spice and mine
   Be where thou left'st them, or lie here with me.
Ask for those kings whom thou saw'st yesterday,
And thou shalt hear, 'All here in one bed lay.'

continues

She is all States, and all Princes, I;
    Nothing else is.
Princes do but play us; compar'd to this,
All honour's mimic; all wealth alchemy.
    Thou Sun art half as happy as we,
    In that the world's contracted thus;
  Thine age asks ease, and since thy duties be
  To warm the world, that's done in warming us.
Shine here to us, and thou art every where;
This bed thy centre is, these walls, thy sphere.

                     JOHN DONNE (1572–1631)

∾ The Triple Fool

I am two fools, I know,
For loving, and for saying so
    In whining poetry;
But where's that wise man, that would not be I,
    If she would not deny?
Then as th' earth's inward narrow crooked lanes
Do purge sea-water's fretful salt away,
    I thought, if I could draw my pains
Through rhyme's vexation, I should them allay.
Grief brought to numbers cannot be so fierce,
For he tames it, that fetters it in verse.

    But when I have done so,
Some man, his art and voice to show,
    Doth set and sing my pain,
And, by delighting many, frees again
    Grief, which verse did restrain.
To Love and Grief tribute of Verse belongs,
But not of such as pleases when 'tis read;
    Both are increased by such songs:
For both their triumphs so are published,
And I, which was two fools, do so grow three;
Who are a little wise, the best fools be.

JOHN DONNE (1572–1631)

To His Mistress Going to Bed

Come, Madam, come, all rest my powers defy,
Until I labour, I in labour lie.
The foe oft-times having the foe in sight,
Is tir'd with standing though he never fight.
Off with that girdle, like heaven's Zone glistering,
But a far fairer world encompassing.
Unpin that spangled breastplate which you wear,
That th'eyes of busy fools may be stopped there.
Unlace yourself, for that harmonious chime,
Tells me from you, that now it is bed time.
Off with that happy busk, which I envy,
That still can be, and still can stand so nigh.
Your gown going off, such beauteous state reveals,
As when from flowery meads th'hill's shadow
    steals.
Off with that wiry Coronet and shew
The hairy Diadem which on you doth grow:
Now off with those shoes, and then safely tread
In this love's hallow'd temple, this soft bed.
In such white robes, heaven's Angels used to be
Received by men; Thou Angel bringst with thee
A heaven like Mahomet's Paradise; and though
Ill spirits walk in white, we easily know,
By this these Angels from an evil sprite,
Those set our hairs, but these our flesh upright.

Licence my roving hands, and let them go,
Before, behind, between, above, below.
O my America! my new-found-land,
My kingdom, safeliest when with one man mann'd,
My Mine of precious stones, My Empirie,
How blest am I in this discovering thee!
To enter in these bonds, is to be free;
Then where my hand is set, my seal shall be.
     Full nakedness! All joys are due to thee,
As souls unbodied, bodies uncloth'd must be,
To taste whole joys. Gems which you women use
Are like Atlanta's balls, cast in men's views,
That when a fool's eye lighteth on a Gem,
His earthly soul may covet theirs, not them.
Like pictures, or like books' gay coverings made
For lay-men, are all women thus array'd;
Themselves are mystic books, which only we
(Whom their imputed grace will dignify)
Must see reveal'd. Then since that I may know;
As liberally, as to a Midwife, shew
Thy self: cast all, yea, this white linen hence,
There is no penance due to innocence.
     To teach thee, I am naked first; why then
What needst thou have more covering than a man.

Woman's Constancy

Now thou hast loved me one whole day,
Tomorrow when thou leav'st, what wilt thou say?
Wilt thou then antedate some new-made vow?
           Or say that now
We are not just those persons which we were?
Or, that oaths made in reverential fear
Of Love, and his wrath, any may forswear?
Or, as true deaths, true marriages untie,
So lovers' contracts, images of those,
Bind but till sleep, death's image, them unloose?
           Or, your own end to justify,
For having purposed change, and falsehood, you
Can have no way but falsehood to be true?
Vain lunatic, against these 'scapes I could
           Dispute, and conquer, if I would,
           Which I abstain to do,
For by tomorrow, I may think so too.

           JOHN DONNE (1572–1631)

❧ At Baia

I should have thought
in a dream you would have brought
some lovely, perilous thing,
orchids piled in a great sheath,
as who would say (in a dream)
I send you this,
who left the blue veins
of your throat unkissed.

Why was it that your hands
(that never took mine)
your hands that I could see
drift over the orchid heads
so carefully,
your hands, so fragile, sure to lift
so gently, the fragile flower stuff—
ah, ah, how was it

You never sent (in a dream)
the very form, the very scent,
not heavy, not sensuous,
but perilous—perilous—
of orchids, piled in a great sheath,

stanza continues

and folded underneath on a bright scroll
some word:

Flower sent to flower;
for white hands, the lesser white,
less lovely of flower leaf,

or

Lover to lover, no kiss,
no touch, but forever and ever this.

A Valediction

If we must part,
   Then let it be like this;
Not heart on heart,
   Nor with the useless anguish of a kiss;
But touch mine hand and say;
'Until tomorrow or some other day,
   If we must part.'

Words are so weak
   When love hath been so strong:
Let silence speak:
   'Life is a little while, and love is long;
A time to sow and reap,
And after harvest a long time to sleep,
   But words are weak.'

ERNEST DOWSON (1867–1900)

Non Sum Qualis Eram Bonae Sub Regno Cynarae

Last night, ah, yesternight, betwixt her lips and
   mine
There fell thy shadow, Cynara! thy breath was shed
Upon my soul between the kisses and the wine;
And I was desolate and sick of an old passion,
   Yea, I was desolate and bowed my head:
I have been faithful to thee, Cynara! in my fashion.

All night upon mine heart I felt her warm heart
   beat,
Night-long within mine arms in love and sleep
   she lay;
Surely the kisses of her bought red mouth were
   sweet;
But I was desolate and sick of an old passion,
   When I awoke and found the dawn was gray:
I have been faithful to thee, Cynara! in my fashion.

I have forgot much, Cynara! gone with the wind,
Flung roses, roses, riotously with the throng,
Dancing, to put thy pale lost lilies out of mind;
But I was desolate and sick of an old passion,

stanza continues

Yea, all the time, because the dance was long:
I have been faithful to thee, Cynara! in my fashion.

I cried for madder music and for stronger wine,
But when the feast is finished and the lamps
    expire,
Then falls thy shadow, Cynara! the night is thine;
And I am desolate and sick of an old passion,
    Yea, hungry for the lips of my desire:
I have been faithful to thee, Cynara! in my fashion.

Vitae Summa Brevis Spem Nos Vetet Incohare Longam

They are not long, the weeping and the laughter,
    Love and desire and hate:
I think they have no portion in us after
    We pass the gate.

They are not long, the days of wine and roses:
    Out of a misty dream
Our path emerges for a while, then closes
    Within a dream.

ERNEST DOWSON (1867–1900)

"Since there's no help, come let us kiss and part—"

Since there's no help, come let us kiss and part—
Nay, I have done, you get no more of me;
And I am glad, yeah, glad with all my heart,
That thus so cleanly I myself can free.
Shake hands for ever, cancel all our vows,
And when we meet at any time again,
Be it not seen in either of our brows
That we one jot of former love retain.
Now at the last gasp of Love's latest breath,
When, his pulse failing, Passion speechless lies,
When Faith is kneeling by his bed of death,
And Innocence is closing up his eyes,
  —Now if thou would'st, when all have given him
    over,
  From death to life thou might'st him yet recover.

"Farewell ungrateful traitor,"

from *THE SPANISH FRYAR*

I

Farewell ungrateful traitor,
   Farewell my perjured swain,
Let never injured creature
   Believe a man again.
The pleasure of possessing
Surpasses all expressing,
But 'tis too short a blessing,
   And love too long a pain.

II

'Tis easy to deceive us
   In pity of your pain,
But when we love you leave us
   To rail at you in vain.
Before we have descried it,
There is no bliss beside it,
But she that once has tried it
   Will never love again.

JOHN DRYDEN (1631–1700)

III

The passion you pretended
   Was only to obtain,
But when the charm is ended
   The charmer you disdain.
Your love by ours we measure
Till we have lost our treasure,
But dying is a pleasure,
   When living is a pain.

～ "After the fiercest pangs of hot desire,"

After the fiercest pangs of hot desire,
   Between Panthea's rising breasts
   His bending head Philander rests,
Though vanquished, yet unknowing to retire,
   Close hugs the charmer, and, ashamed to yield,
   Though he has lost the day, still keeps the field.

When, with a sigh, the fair Panthea said,
   'What pity 'tis, ye gods, that all
   The bravest warriors soonest fall!'
Then, with a kiss, she gently raised his head,
   Armed him again for fight, for nobly she
   More loved the combat than the victory.

Then, more enraged for being beat before,
   With all his strength he does prepare
   More fiercely to renew the war;
Nor ceases till that noble prize he bore;
   Even her such wonderous courage did surprise;
   She hugs the dart that wounded her, and dies.

RICHARD DUKE (1658?–1711)

Epitaph on the Monument of
Sir William Dyer at Colmworth, 1641

My dearest dust, could not thy hasty day
Afford thy drowsy patience leave to stay
One hour longer: so that we might either
Sit up, or gone to bed together?
But since thy finished labour hath possessed
Thy weary limbs with early rest,
Enjoy it sweetly: and thy widow bride
Shall soon repose her by thy slumbering side.
Whose business, now, is only to prepare
My nightly dress, and call to prayer:
Mine eyes wax heavy and the day grows old,
The dew falls thick, my blood grows cold.
Draw, draw the closéd curtains: and make room:
My dear, my dearest dust; I come, I come.

❧ A Silent Love

The lowest trees have tops, the ant her gall,
The fly her spleen, the little spark his heat;
The slender hairs cast shadows, though but small,
And bees have stings, although they be not great;
  Seas have their source, and so have shallow
    springs;
  And love is love, in beggars and in kings.

Where waters smoothest run, there deepest are
  the fords,
The dial stirs, yet none perceives it move;
The firmest faith is found in fewest words,
The turtles do not sing, and yet they love;
  True hearts have ears and eyes, no tongues
    to speak;
  They hear and see, and sigh, and then they
    break.

SIR EDWARD DYER (1543?–1607)

❧ "When I was fair and young and favour gracèd me,"

When I was fair and young and favour gracèd me,
Of many was I sought, their mistress for to be:
But I did scorn them all, and answered them
        therefore,
  'Go, go, go, seek some other where:
        Importune me no more.'

How many weeping eyes I made to pine with woe,
How many sighing hearts, I have no skill to show:
Yet I the prouder grew, and answered them
        therefore,
  'Go, go, go, seek some other where:
        Importune me no more.'

Then spake fair Venus' son, that proud victorious
        boy,
And said, 'Fine Dame, since that you be so coy,
I will so pluck your plumes that you shall say
        no more,
  'Go, go, go, seek some other where:
        Importune me no more.'

continues

When he had spake these words, such change grew
      in my breast
That neither night nor day, since that, I could take
      any rest:
Than lo, I did repent that I had said before,
  'Go, go, go, seek some other where:
        Importune me no more.'

❧ Love's Emblems

Now the lusty spring is seen;
  Golden yellow, gaudy blue,
  Daintily invite the view:
Everywhere on every green
Roses blushing as they blow
  And enticing men to pull,
Lilies whiter than the snow,
   Woodbines of sweet honey full:
    All love's emblems, and all cry,
    'Ladies, if not plucked, we die.'

Yet the lusty spring hath stayed;
  Blushing red and purest white
  Daintily to love invite
Every woman, every maid:
Cherries kissing as they grow,
  And inviting men to taste,
Apples even ripe below,
   Winding gently to the waist:
    All love's emblems, and all cry,
    'Ladies, if not plucked, we die.'

Take, Oh, Take Those Lips Away

Take, oh, take those lips away
That so sweetly were forsworn
And those eyes, like break of day,
Lights that do mislead the morn;
But my kisses bring again,
Seals of love, though sealed in vain.

Hide, oh, hide those hills of snow,
Which thy frozen bosom bears,
On whose tops the pinks that grow
Are of those that April wears;
But first set my poor heart free,
Bound in those icy chains by thee.

Meeting and Passing

As I went down the hill along the wall
There was a gate I had leaned at for the view
And had just turned from when I first saw you
As you came up the hill. We met. But all
We did that day was mingle great and small
Footprints in summer dust as if we drew
The figure of our being less than two
But more than one as yet. Your parasol
Pointed the decimal off with one deep thrust.
And all the time we talked you seemed to see
Something down there to smile at in the dust.
(Oh, it was without prejudice to me!)
Afterward I went past what you had passed
Before we met, and you what I had passed.

When Lovely Woman Stoops to Folly

When lovely woman stoops to folly,
    And finds too late that men betray,
What charm can soothe her melancholy,
    What art can wash her guilt away?

The only art her guilt to cover,
    To hide her shame from every eye,
To give repentance to her love,
    And wring his bosom—is to die.

Love

Love is begot by fancy, bred
  By ignorance, by expectation fed,
Destroyed by knowledge, and, at best,
Lost in the moment 'tis possessed.

❧ A Kiss

By a wall the stranger now calls his,
Was born of old a particular kiss,
Without forethought in its genesis;
Which in a trice took wing on the air.
And where that spot is nothing shows:
    There ivy calmly grows,
    And no one knows
    What a birth was there!

That kiss is gone where none can tell—
Not even those who felt its spell:
It cannot have died; that know we well.
Somewhere it pursues its flight,
One of a long procession of sounds
    Travelling aethereal rounds
    Far from earth's bounds
    In the infinite.

       THOMAS HARDY (1840–1928)

❧ A Week

On Monday night I closed my door,
And thought you were not as heretofore,
And little cared if we met no more.

I seemed on Tuesday night to trace
Something beyond mere commonplace
In your ideas, and heart, and face.

On Wednesday I did not opine
Your life would ever be one with mine,
Though if it were we should well combine.

On Thursday noon I liked you well,
And fondly felt that we must dwell
Not far apart, whatever befell.

On Friday it was with a thrill
In gazing towards your distant vill
I owned you were my dear one still.

I saw you wholly to my mind
On Saturday—even one who shrined
All that was best of womankind.

continues

As wing-clipt sea-gull for the sea
On Sunday night I longed for thee,
Without whom life were waste to me!

THOMAS HARDY (1840–1928)

The Sigh

Little head against my shoulder,
Shy at first, then somewhat bolder,
    And up-eyed;
Till she, with a timid quaver,
Yielded to the kiss I gave her;
    But, she sighed.

That there mingled with her feeling
Some sad thought she was concealing
    It implied.
—Not that she had ceased to love me,
None on earth she set above me;
    But she sighed.

She could not disguise a passion,
Dread, or doubt, in weakest fashion
    If she tried:
Nothing seemed to hold us sundered,
Hearts were victors; so I wondered
    Why she sighed.

Afterwards I knew her throughly,
And she loved me staunchly, truly,
    Till she died;

stanza continues

But she never made confession
Why, at that first sweet concession,
　　She had sighed.

It was in our May, remember;
And though now I near November,
　　And abide
Till my appointed change, unfretting,
Sometimes I sit half regretting
　　That she sighed.

❧ The Voice

Woman much missed, how you call to me, call
   to me,
Saying that now you are not as you were
When you had changed from the one who was all
   to me,
But as at first, when our day was fair.

Can it be you that I hear? Let me view you, then,
Standing as when I drew near to the town
Where you would wait for me: yes, as I knew
   you then,
Even to the original air-blue gown!

Or is it only the breeze in its listlessness
Travelling across the wet mead to me here,
You being ever dissolved to wan wistlessness,
Heard no more again far or near?

   Thus I; faltering forward,
   Leaves around me falling,
Wind oozing thin through the thorn from norward,
   And the woman calling.

Of an Heroical Answer of a Great Roman Lady to Her Husband

A grave wise man that had a great rich lady,
Such as perhaps in these days found there may be,
Did think she played him false and more than think,
Save that in wisdom he thereat did wink.
Howbeit one time disposed to sport and play
Thus to his wife he pleasantly did say,
'Since strangers lodge their arrows in thy quiver,
Dear dame, I pray you yet the cause deliver,
If you can tell the cause and not dissemble,
How all our children me so much resemble?'
The lady blushed but yet this answer made
'Though I have used some traffic in the trade,
And must confess, as you have touched before,
My bark was sometimes steered with foreign oar,
    Yet stowed I no man's stuff but first persuaded
    The bottom with your ballast full was laded.'

The Author to His Wife,
of a Woman's Eloquence

My Mall, I mark that when you mean to prove me
To buy a velvet gown, or some rich border,
Thou call'st me good sweet heart, thou swear'st to
    love me,
Thy locks, thy lips, thy looks, speak all in order,
Thou think'st, and right thou think'st, that these do
    move me,
That all these severally thy suit do further:
    But shall I tell thee what most thy suit advances?
    Thy fair smooth words? no, no, thy fair smooth
      haunches.

❧ Love

Love bade me welcome: yet my soul drew back,
    Guilty of dust and sin.
But quick-eyed Love, observing me grow slack
    From my first entrance in,
Drew nearer to me, sweetly questioning
    If I lacked any thing.

"A guest," I answered, "worthy to be here":
    Love said, "You shall be he."
"I, the unkind, ungrateful? Ah, my dear,
    I cannot look on thee."
Love took my hand, and smiling did reply,
    "Who made the eyes but I?"

"Truth, Lord; but I have marred them; let
    my shame
        Go where it doth deserve."
"And know you not," says Love, "who bore
    the blame?"
        "My dear, then I will serve."
"You must sit down," says Love, "and taste
    my meat."
        So I did sit and eat.

❦ Corinna's Going A-Maying

Get up! get up for shame! the blooming morn
Upon her wings presents the god unshorn.
  See how Aurora throws her fair
  Fresh-quilted colors through the air:
  Get up, sweet slug-a-bed, and see
  The dew bespangling herb and tree.
Each flower has wept and bowèd toward the east
Above an hour since, yet you not dressed;
  Nay, not so much as out of bed?
  When all the birds have matins said,
  And sung their thankful hymns, 'tis sin,
  Nay, profanation to keep in,
Whenas a thousand virgins on this day
Spring, sooner than the lark, to fetch in May.

Rise, and put on your foliage, and be seen
To come forth, like the springtime, fresh and green,
  And sweet as Flora. Take no care
  For jewels for your gown or hair;
  Fear not; the leaves will strew
  Gems in abundance upon you;
Besides, the childhood of the day has kept,
Against you come, some orient pearls unwept;

stanza continues

ROBERT HERRICK (1591–1674)   113

Come and receive them while the light
Hangs on the dew-locks of the night,
And Titan on the eastern hill
Retires himself, or else stands still
Till you come forth. Wash, dress, be brief in praying:
Few beads are best when once we go a-Maying.

Come, my Corinna, come; and, coming mark
How each field turns a street, each street a park
Made green and trimmed with trees; see how
Devotion gives each house a bough
Or branch: each porch, each door ere this,
An ark, a tabernacle is,
Made up of whitethorn neatly interwove,
As if here were those cooler shades of love.
Can such delights be in the street
And open fields, and we not see 't?
Come, we'll abroad; and let's obey
The proclamation made for May,
And sin no more, as we have done, by staying;
But, my Corinna, come, let's go a-Maying.

There's not a budding boy or girl this day
But is got up and gone to bring in May;
A deal of youth, ere this, is come
Back, and with whitethorn laden home.

stanza continues

Some have dispatched their cakes and cream
   Before that we have left to dream;
And some have wept, and wooed, and plighted
   troth,
And chose their priest, ere we can cast off sloth.
   Many a green-gown has been given,
   Many a kiss, both odd and even,
   Many a glance, too, has been sent
   From out the eye, love's firmament;
Many a jest told of the keys betraying
This night, and locks picked; yet we're not
   a-Maying.

Come, let us go while we are in our prime,
And take the harmless folly of the time.
   We shall grow old apace, and die
   Before we know our liberty.
   Our life is short, and our days run
   As fast away as does the sun;
And, as a vapor or a drop of rain
Once lost, can ne'er be found again;
   So when or you or I are made
   A fable, song, or fleeting shade,
   All love, all liking, all delight
   Lies drowned with us in endless night.
Then while time serves, and we are but decaying,
Come, my Corinna, come, let's go a-Maying.

❧ Delight in Disorder

A sweet disorder in the dress
Kindles in clothes a wantonness.
A lawn about the shoulders thrown
Into a fine distractiòn;
An erring lace, which here and there
Enthralls the crimson stomacher;
A cuff neglectful, and thereby
Ribbons to flow confusedly;
A winning wave, deserving note,
In the tempestuous petticoat;
A careless shoestring, in whose tie
I see a wild civility;
Do more bewitch me than when art
Is too precise in every part.

ROBERT HERRICK (1591–1674)

The Vine

I dreamed this mortal part of mine
Was metamorphosed to a vine,
Which crawling one and every way
Enthralled my dainty Lucia.
Methought her long small legs and thighs
I with my tendrils did surprise;
Her belly, buttocks, and her waist
By my soft nervelets were embraced.
About her head I writhing hung,
And with rich clusters (hid among
The leaves) her temples I behung,
So that my Lucia seemed to me
Young Bacchus ravished by his tree.
My curls about her neck did crawl,
And arms and hands they did enthrall,
So that she could not freely stir
(All parts there made one prisoner).
But when I crept with leaves to hide
Those parts which maids keep unespied,
Such fleeting pleasures there I took
That with the fancy I awoke;
And found (ah me!) this flesh of mine
More like a stock than like a vine.

ROBERT HERRICK (1591–1674)

To the Virgins, to Make Much of Time

Gather ye rosebuds while ye may,
    Old Time is still a-flying:
And this same flower that smiles today
    Tomorrow will be dying.

The glorious lamp of heaven, the sun,
    The higher he's a-getting,
The sooner will his race be run,
    And nearer he's to setting.

That age is best which is the first,
    When youth and blood are warmer;
But being spent, the worse, and worst
    Times still succeed the former.

Then be not coy, but use your time,
    And while ye may, go marry:
For having lost but once your prime,
    You may for ever tarry.

ROBERT HERRICK (1591–1674)

Upon Julia's Clothes

When as in silks my Julia goes,
    Then, then (methinks) how sweetly flows
That liquefaction of her clothes.

Next, when I cast mine eyes and see
That brave vibration each way free;
    O how that glittering taketh me!

❧ "Oh, when I was in love with you,"

Oh, when I was in love with you,
   Then I was clean and brave,
And miles around the wonder grew
   How well did I behave.

And now the fancy passes by,
   And nothing will remain,
And miles around they'll say that I
   Am quite myself again.

A. E. HOUSMAN (1859–1936)

❧ Fain Would I Change That Note

Fain would I change that note
  To which fond Love hath charmed me
Long, long to sing by rote,
Fancying that that harm'd me.
Yet when this thought doth come,
'Love is the perfect sum
  Of all delight.'
I have no other choice
Either for pen or voice
  To sing or write.

O love, they wrong thee much
That say thy sweet is bitter,
When thy rich fruit is such
As nothing can be sweeter.
Fair house of joy and bliss,
Where truest pleasure is,
  I do adore thee:
I know thee what thou art,
I serve thee with my heart,
  And fall before thee.

CAPTAIN TOBIAS HUME (1569?–1645)   121

Jenny Kiss'd Me

Jenny kiss'd me when we met,
   Jumping from the chair she sat in;
Time, you thief, who love to get
   Sweets into your list, put that in!
Say I'm weary, say I'm sad,
   Say that health and wealth have miss'd me,
Say I'm growing old, but add,
   Jenny kiss'd me.

          LEIGH HUNT (1784–1859)

❧ Though I Am Young and Cannot Tell

Though I am young, and cannot tell
   Either what Death or Love is well,
Yet I have heard they both bear darts,
   And both do aim at human hearts.
And then again, I have been told
   Love wounds with heat, as Death with cold;
So that I fear they do but bring
   Extremes to touch, and mean one thing.

As in a ruin we it call
   One thing to be blown up, or fall;
Or to our end like way may have
   By a flash of lightning, or a wave;
So Love's inflamèd shaft or brand
   May kill as soon as Death's cold hand;
Except Love's fires the virtue have
   To fright the frost out of the grave.

BEN JONSON (1572–1637)

❧ To Celia

Drink to me only with thine eyes,
   And I will pledge with mine;
Or leave a kiss but in the cup
   And I'll not look for wine.
The thirst that from the soul doth rise
   Doth ask a drink divine;
But might I of Jove's nectar sup,
   I would not change for thine.
I sent thee late a rosy wreath,
   Not so much honouring thee
As giving it a hope that there
   I could not withered be;
But thou thereon didst only breathe,
   And sent'st it back to me;
Since when it grows, and smells, I swear,
   Not of itself but thee!

       BEN JONSON (1572–1637)

❧ Chamber Music XIII

Go seek her out all courteously,
   And say I come,
Wind of spices whose song is ever
   Epithalamium.
O, hurry over the dark lands
   And run upon the sea
For seas and land shall not divide us
   My love and me.

Now, wind, of your good courtesy
   I pray you go,
And come into her little garden
   And sing at her window;
Singing: The bridal wind is blowing
   For Love is at his noon;
And soon will your true love be with you,
   Soon, O soon.

Chamber Music XX

In the dark pine-wood
   I would we lay,
In deep cool shadow
   At noon of day.

How sweet to lie there,
   Sweet to kiss,
Where the great pine-forest
   Enaisled is!

Thy kiss descending
   Sweeter were
With a soft tumult
   Of thy hair.

O, unto the pine-wood
   At noon of day
Come with me now,
   Sweet love, away.

JAMES JOYCE (1882–1941)

Bright Star

Bright Star, would I were steadfast as thou art—
Not in lone splendour hung aloft the night,
And watching, with eternal lids apart,
Like Nature's patient sleepless Eremite,
The moving waters at their priest-like task
Of pure ablution round earth's human shores,
Or gazing on the new soft-fallen mask
Of snow upon the mountains and the moors—
No—yet still steadfast, still unchangeable,
Pillow'd upon my fair love's ripening breast,
To feel for ever its soft fall and swell,
Awake for ever in a sweet unrest,
Still, still to hear her tender-taken breath,
And so live ever—or else swoon to death.

JOHN KEATS (1795–1821)   127

"I cry your mercy—pity—love!— aye, love!"

I cry your mercy—pity—love!—aye, love!
  Merciful love that tantalizes not,
One-thoughted, never-wandering, guileless love,
  Unmasked, and being seen—without a blot!
O! let me have thee whole,—all—all—be mine!
  That shape, that fairness, that sweet minor zest
Of love, your kiss,—those hands, those eyes divine,
  That warm, white, lucent, million-pleasured
    breast,—
Yourself—your soul—in pity give me all,
  Withhold no atom's atom or I die,
Or living on perhaps, your wretched thrall,
  Forget, in the mist of idle misery,
Life's purposes,—the palate of my mind
Losing its gust, and my ambition blind!

La Belle Dame sans Merci

O what can ail thee, Knight at arms,
　Alone and palely loitering?
The sedge has withered from the Lake
　And no birds sing!

O what can ail thee, Knight at arms,
　So haggard, and so woebegone?
The squirrel's granary is full
　And the harvest's done.

I see a lily on thy brow
　With anguish moist and fever dew,
And on thy cheeks a fading rose
　Fast withereth too.

"I met a Lady in the Meads,
　Full beautiful, a faery's child,
Her hair was long, her foot was light
　And her eyes were wild.

"I made a Garland for her head,
　And bracelets too, and fragrant Zone;
She looked at me as she did love
　And made sweet moan.

continues

JOHN KEATS (1795–1821)

"I set her on my pacing steed
    And nothing else saw all day long,
For sidelong would she bend and sing
    A faery's song.

"She found me roots of relish sweet,
    And honey wild, and manna dew,
And sure in language strange she said
    'I love thee true.'

"She took me to her elfin grot
    And there she wept and sighed full sore,
And there I shut her wild wild eyes
    With kisses four.

"And there she lullèd me asleep,
    And there I dreamed, Ah Woe betide!
The latest dream I ever dreamt
    On the cold hill side.

"I saw pale Kings, and Princes too,
    Pale warriors, death-pale were they all;
They cried, 'La belle dame sans merci
    Hath thee in thrall!'

"I saw their starved lips in the gloam
  With horrid warning gapèd wide,
And I awoke, and found me here
  On the cold hill's side.

"And this is why I sojourn here,
  Alone and palely loitering;
Though the sedge is withered from the Lake
  And no birds sing."

❧ "This living hand, now warm and capable"

This living hand, now warm and capable
Of earnest grasping, would, if it were cold
And in the icy silence of the tomb,
So haunt thy days and chill thy dreaming nights
That thou wouldst wish thine own heart dry
    of blood
So in my veins red life might stream again,
And thou be conscience-calmed—see here it is—
I hold it towards you.

JOHN KEATS (1795–1821)

❧ "Ah Love! could thou and I
with Fate conspire"

from *THE RUBÁIYÁT*

Ah Love! could thou and I with Fate conspire
To grasp this sorry Scheme of Things entire,
   Would not we shatter it to bits—and then
Re-mould it nearer to the Heart's Desire!

Translated from the Persian by
Edward Fitzgerald (1809–1883)

❧ "Here with a Loaf of Bread beneath the Bough,"

from *THE RUBÁIYÁT*

Here with a Loaf of Bread beneath the Bough,
A Flask of Wine, a Book of Verse—and Thou
    Beside me singing in the Wilderness—
And Wilderness is Paradise enow.

Translated from the Persian by
Edward Fitzgerald (1809–1883)

OMAR KHAYYÁM (11TH CENTURY)

Rose Aylmer

Ah what avails the sceptered race,
  Ah what the form divine!
What every virtue, every grace!
  Rose Aylmer, all were thine.
Rose Aylmer, whom these wakeful eyes
  May weep, but never see,
A night of memories and of sighs
  I consecrate to thee.

"You smiled, you spoke, and I believed,"

You smiled, you spoke, and I believed,
By every word and smile deceived.
Another man would hope no more;
Nor hope I what I hoped before:
But let not this last wish be vain;
Deceive, deceive me once again!

❧ The Fan

For various purpose serves the fan,
   As thus—a decent blind,
Between the sticks to peep at man,
   Nor yet betray your mind.

Each action has a meaning plain:
   Resentment's in the snap;
A flirt expresses strong disdain,
   Consent a tiny tap.

All passions will the fan disclose,
   All modes of female art;
And to advantage sweetly shews
   The hand if not the heart.

'Tis Folly's sceptre, first design'd
   By Love's capricious boy,
Who knows how lightly all mankind
   Are govern'd by a toy.

ROBERT LLOYD (1733–1764)

The Scrutiny

Why should you swear I am forsworn,
  Since thine I vowed to be?
Lady it is already morn,
  And 'twas last night I swore to thee
That fond impossibility.

Have I not loved thee much and long,
  A tedious twelve hours' space?
I must all other Beauties wrong,
  And rob thee of a new embrace;
Could I still dote upon thy face.

Not, but all joy in thy brown hair,
  By others may be found;
But I must search the black and fair
  Like skilful mineralists that sound
For treasure in un-plowed-up ground.

Then, if when I have loved my round,
  Thou provest the pleasant she;
With spoils of meaner Beauties crowned,
  I laden will return to thee,
Ev'n sated with variety.

To Lucasta, Going to the Wars

Tell me not, sweet, I am unkind,
That from the nunnery
Of thy chaste breast and quiet mind,
To war and arms I fly.

True, a new mistress now I chase,
The first foe in the field;
And with a stronger faith embrace
A sword, a horse, a shield.

Yet this inconstancy is such
As you too shall adore;
I could not love thee, dear, so much,
Loved I not honor more.

RICHARD LOVELACE (1618–1657)

"When Delia on the plain appears,"

When Delia on the plain appears,
Aw'd by a thousand tender fears,
I would approach, but dare not move;
Tell me, my heart, if this be love?

Whene'er she speaks, my ravish'd ear
No other voice but her's can hear,
No other wit but her's approve;
Tell me, my heart, if this be love?

If she some other youth commend,
Though I was once his fondest friend,
His instant enemy I prove;
Tell me, my heart, if this be love?

When she is absent, I no more
Delight in all that pleas'd before,
The clearest spring, or shadiest grove;
Tell me, my heart, if this be love?

When fond of pow'r, of beauty vain,
Her nets she spreads for ev'ry swain,
I strove to hate, but vainly strove;
Tell me, my heart, if this be love?

"In summer's heat and mid-time of the day"

from OVID'S *ELEGIES*

In summer's heat and mid-time of the day
To rest my limbs upon a bed I lay,
One window shut, the other open stood,
Which gave such light as twinkles in a wood,
Like twilight glimpse at setting of the sun
Or night being past, and yet not day begun.
Such light to shamefaced maidens must be shown,
Where they may sport, and seem to be unknown.
Then came Corinna in a long loose gown,
Her white neck hid with tresses hanging down:
Resembling fair Semiramis going to bed
Or Laïs of a thousand wooers sped.
I snatched her gown, being thin, the harm was small,
Yet strived she to be covered therewithal.
And striving thus as one that would be cast,
Betrayed herself, and yielded at the last.
Stark naked as she stood before mine eye,
Not one wen in her body could I spy.
What arms and shoulders did I touch and see,
How apt her breasts were to be pressed by me?

continues

CHRISTOPHER MARLOWE (1564–1593)

How smooth a belly under her waist saw I?
How large a leg, and what a lusty thigh?
To leave the rest, all liked me passing well,
I clinged her naked body, down she fell,
Judge you the rest: being tired she bad me kiss,
Jove send me more such afternoons as this.

Translated from the Latin

The Passionate Shepherd to His Love

Come live with me and be my Love,
And we will all the pleasures prove
That hills and valleys, dales and fields,
Or woods or steepy mountain yields.

And we will sit upon the rocks,
And see the shepherds feed their flocks
By shallow rivers, to whose falls
Melodious birds sing madrigals.

And I will make thee beds of roses
And a thousand fragrant posies;
A cap of flowers, and a kirtle —
Embroidered all with leaves of myrtle.

A gown made of the finest wool
Which from our pretty lambs we pull;
Fair-linèd slippers for the cold,
With buckles of the purest gold.

A belt of straw and ivy-buds
With coral clasps and amber studs:
And if these pleasures may thee move,
Come live with me and be my Love.

continues

CHRISTOPHER MARLOWE (1564–1593)   143

The shepherd swains shall dance and sing
For thy delight each May morning:
If these delights thy mind may move,
Then live with me and be my Love.

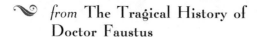

from The Tragical History of Doctor Faustus

Was this the face that launch'd a thousand ships,
And burnt the topless towers of Ilium?—
Sweet Helen, make me immortal with a kiss.—
Her lips suck forth my soul: see, where it flies!—
Come, Helen, come, give me my soul again.
Here will I dwell, for heaven is in these lips,
And all is dross that is not Helena.
I will be Paris, and for love of thee,
Instead of Troy, shall Wertenberg be sack'd;
And I will combat with weak Menelaus,
And wear thy colours on my plumed crest;
Yes, I will wound Achilles in the heel,
And then return to Helen for a kiss.
O, thou art fairer than the evening air
Clad in the beauty of a thousand stars;
Brighter art thou than flaming Jupiter
When he appear'd to hapless Semele;
More lovely than the monarch of the sky
In wanton Arethusa's azur'd arms;
And none but thou shalt be my paramour!

The Definition of Love

My Love is of a birth as rare
As 'tis for object strange and high:
It was begotten by Despair
Upon Impossibility.

Magnanimous Despair alone
Could show me so divine a thing,
Where feeble Hope could ne'er have flown
But vainly flapped its tinsel wing.

And yet I quickly might arrive
Where my extended soul is fixed,
But Fate does iron wedges drive,
And always crowds itself betwixt.

For Fate with jealous eye does see
Two perfect Loves; nor lets them close:
Their union would her ruin be,
And her tyrannic power depose.

And therefore her decrees of steel
Us as the distant Poles have placed,
(Though Love's whole World on us doth wheel)
Not by themselves to be embraced.

ANDREW MARVELL (1621–1678)

Unless the giddy Heaven fall,
And Earth some new convulsion tear;
And, us to join, the World should all
Be cramped into a planisphere.

As lines so Love oblique may well
Themselves in every angle greet:
But ours so truly parallel,
Though infinite, can never meet.

Therefore the Love which us doth bind
But Fate so enviously debars,
Is the conjunction of the Mind,
And opposition of the Stars.

❧ To His Coy Mistress

Had we but world enough, and time,
This coyness, Lady, were no crime.
We would sit down and think which way
To walk and pass our long love's day.
Thou by the Indian Ganges' side
Shouldst rubies find: I by the tide
Of Humber would complain. I would
Love you ten years before the Flood,
And you should, if you please, refuse
Till the conversion of the Jews.
My vegetable love should grow
Vaster than empires, and more slow;
An hundred years should go to praise
Thine eyes and on thy forehead gaze;
Two hundred to adore each breast;
But thirty thousand to the rest;
An age at least to every part,
And the last age should show your heart;
For, Lady, you deserve this state,
Nor would I love at lower rate.
    But at my back I always hear
Time's wingèd chariot hurrying near;
And yonder all before us lie
Deserts of vast eternity.

Thy beauty shall no more be found,
Nor, in thy marble vault, shall sound
My echoing song: then worms shall try
That long preserved virginity,
And your quaint honour turn to dust,
And into ashes all my lust:
The grave's a fine and private place,
But none, I think, do there embrace.
  Now therefore, while the youthful hue
Sits on thy skin like morning dew,
And while thy willing soul transpires
At every pore with instant fires,
Now let us sport us while we may,
And now, like amorous birds of prey,
Rather at once our time devour
Than languish in his slow-chapt power.
Let us roll all our strength and all
Our sweetness up into one ball,
And tear our pleasures with rough strife
Thorough the iron gates of life:
Thus, though we cannot make our sun
Stand still, yet we will make him run.

❦ Modern Love XVI

In our old shipwrecked days there was an hour,
When in the firelight steadily aglow,
Joined slackly, we beheld the red chasm grow
Among the clicking coals. Our library-bower
That eve was left to us: and hushed we sat
As lovers to whom Time is whispering.
From sudden-opened doors we heard them sing:
The nodding elders mixed good wine with chat.
Well knew we that Life's greatest treasure lay
With us, and of it was our talk. 'Ah, yes!
Love dies!' I said: I never thought it less.
She yearned to me that sentence to unsay.
Then when the fire domed blackening, I found
Her cheek was salt against my kiss, and swift
Up the sharp scale of sobs her breast did lift:—
Now am I haunted by that taste! that sound!

GEORGE MEREDITH (1828–1909)

Modern Love XVII

At dinner, she is hostess, I am host.
Went the feast ever cheerfuller? She keeps
The Topic over intellectual deeps
In buoyancy afloat. They see no ghost.
With sparkling surface-eyes we ply the ball:
It is in truth a most contagious game:
HIDING THE SKELETON, shall be its name.
Such play as this the devils might appal!
But here's the greater wonder: in that we,
Enamoured of an acting nought can tire,
Each other, like true hypocrites, admire;
Warm-lighted looks, Love's ephemerioe,
Shoot gaily o'er the dishes and the wine.
We waken envy of our happy lot.
Fast, sweet, and golden, shows the marriage-knot.
Dear guests, you now have seen Love's corpse-
  light shine.

GEORGE MEREDITH (1828–1909)

❧ Renouncement

I must not think of thee; and, tired yet strong,
I shun the thought that lurks in all delight—
    The thought of thee—and in the blue heaven's
        height,
And in the sweetest passage of a song.
Oh, just beyond the fairest thoughts that throng
    This breast, the thought of thee waits hidden
        yet bright;
But it must never, never come in sight;
I must stop short of thee the whole day long.
But when sleep comes to close each difficult day,
    When night gives pause to the long watch I keep,
And all my bonds I needs must loose apart,
Must doff my will as raiment laid away,—
    With the first dream that comes with the
        first sleep
I run, I run, I am gathered to thy heart.

ALICE MEYNELL (1847–1922)

"What lips my lips have kissed, and where, and why,"

What lips my lips have kissed, and where, and why,
I have forgotten, and what arms have lain
Under my head till morning; but the rain
Is full of ghosts tonight, that tap and sigh
Upon the glass and listen for reply,
And in my heart there stirs a quiet pain
For unremembered lads that not again
Will turn to me at midnight with a cry.
Thus in the winter stands the lonely tree,
Nor knows what birds have vanished one by one,
Yet knows its boughs more silent than before:
I cannot say what loves have come and gone;
I only know that summer sang in me
A little while, that in me sings no more.

❧ Sonnet XXIII

Methought I saw my late espousèd saint
   Brought to me like Alcestis from the grave,
   Whom Jove's great son to her glad husband
     gave,
   Rescued from death by force though pale and
     faint.
Mine as whom washed from spot of childbed taint,
   Purification in the old Law did save,
   And such, as yet once more I trust to have
   Full sight of her in Heaven without restraint,
Came vested all in white, pure as her mind:
   Her face was veiled, yet to my fancied sight,
   Love, sweetness, goodness, in her person shined
So clear, as in no face with more delight.
   But O as to embrace me she inclined
   I waked, she fled, and day brought back my
     night.

❦ An Argument

I've oft been told by learned friars,
   That wishing and the crime are one,
And Heaven punishes desires
   As much as if the deed were done.

If wishing damns us, you and I
   Are damned to all our heart's content;
Come, then, at least we may enjoy
   Some pleasure for our punishment!

❧ Did Not

'Twas a new feeling—something more
Than we had dared to own before,
   Which then we hid not;
We saw it in each other's eye,
And wished, in every half-breathed sigh,
   To speak, but did not.

She felt my lips' impassioned touch—
'Twas the first time I dared so much,
   And yet she chid not;
But whispered o'er my burning brow,
'Oh, do you doubt I love you now?'
   Sweet soul! I did not.

Warmly I felt her bosom thrill,
I pressed it closer, closer still,
   Though gently bid not;
Till—oh! the world hath seldom heard
Of lovers, who so nearly erred,
   And yet, who did not.

THOMAS MOORE (1779–1852)

Love, That Doth Reign and Live Within My Thought

Love, that doth reign and live within my thought,
And built his seat within my captive breast,
Clad in the arms wherein with me he fought,
Oft in my face he doth his banner rest.
But she that taught me love and suffer pain,
My doubtful hope and eke my hot desire
With shamefast look to shadow and refrain,
Her smiling grace converteth straight to ire.
And coward Love, then, to the heart apace
Taketh his flight, where he doth lurk and plain,
His purpose lost, and dare not show his face.
For my lord's guilt thus faultless bide I pain,
Yet from my lord shall not my foot remove:
Sweet is the death that taketh end by love.

Translated from the Italian by
Henry Howard, Earl of Surrey (1517?–1547)

The Long Love, That in My Thought Doth Harbor

The long love, that in my thought doth harbor,
   And in mine heart doth keep his residence,
   Into my face presseth with bold pretense,
   And therein campeth, spreading his banner.
She that me learneth to love and suffer,
   And wills that my trust and lust's negligence
   Be reined by reason, shame and reverence,
   With his hardiness taketh displeasure.
Wherewithal, unto the heart's forest he fleeth,
   Leaving his enterprise with pain and cry;
   And there him hideth, and not appeareth.
What may I do when my master feareth
   But in the field with him to live and die?
   For good is the life, ending faithfully.

Translated from the Italian by
Sir Thomas Wyatt (1503–1542)

"Whoso list to hunt, I know where is an hind,"

Whoso list to hunt, I know where is an hind,
But as for me, alas, I may no more
The vain travail hath wearied me so sore.
I am of them that farthest cometh behind;
Yet may I by no means my wearied mind
Draw from the Deer: but as she fleeth afore,
Fainting I follow. I leave off therefore,
Since in a net I seek to hold the wind.
Who list her hunt, I put him out of doubt,
As well as I may spend his time in vain:
And, graven with diamonds, in letters plain
There is written her fair neck round about:
Noli me tangere, for Caesar's I am;
And wild for to hold, though I seem tame.

Translated from the Italian by
Sir Thomas Wyatt (1503–1542)

❧ "Doing, a filthy pleasure is, and short;"

Doing, a filthy pleasure is, and short;
And done, we straight repent us of the sport:
Let us not then rush blindly on unto it,
Like lustful beasts, that only know to do it:
For lust will languish, and that heat decay.
But thus, thus, keeping endless holiday,
Let us together closely lie and kiss,
There is no labour, nor no shame in this;
This hath pleased, doth please, and long will
   please; never
Can this decay, but is beginning ever.

Translated from the Latin by
Ben Jonson (1572–1637)

To Mrs M.A. Upon Absence

'Tis now since I began to die
   Four months, yet still I gasping live;
Wrapp'd up in sorrow do I lie,
   Hoping, yet doubting a reprieve.
Adam from Paradise expell'd
Just such a wretched being held.

'Tis not thy love I fear to lose,
   That will in spite of absence hold;
But 'tis the benefit and use
   Is lost, as in imprison'd gold:
Which though the sum be ne'er so great,
Enriches nothing but conceit.

What angry star then governs me
   That I must feel a double smart,
Prisoner to fate as well as thee;
   Kept from thy face, link'd to thy heart?
Because my love all love excels,
Must my grief have no parallels?

Sapless and dead as Winter here
   I now remain, and all I see
Copies of my wild state appear,

stanza continues

But I am their epitome.
Love me no more, for I am grown
Too dead and dull for thee to own.

❧ Annabel Lee

It was many and many a year ago,
    In a kingdom by the sea,
That a maiden there lived whom you may know
    By the name of Annabel Lee;
And this maiden she lived with no other thought
    Than to love and be loved by me.

She was a child and *I* was a child,
    In this kingdom by the sea,
But we loved with a love that was more than
    love—
    I and my Annabel Lee—
With a love that the wingèd seraphs of Heaven
    Coveted her and me.

And this was the reason that, long ago,
    In this kingdom by the sea,
A wind blew out of a cloud by night
    Chilling my Annabel Lee;
So that her highborn kinsmen came
    And bore her away from me,
To shut her up in a sepulchre
    In this kingdom by the sea.

continues

The angels, not half so happy in Heaven,
    Went envying her and me:
Yes! that was the reason (as all men know,
    In this kingdom by the sea)
That the wind came out of the cloud, chilling
    And killing my Annabel Lee.

But our love it was stronger by far than the love
    Of those who were older than we—
    Of many far wiser than we—
And neither the angels in Heaven above
    Nor the demons down under the sea,
Can ever dissever my soul from the soul
    Of the beautiful Annabel Lee:

For the moon never beams without bringing me
  dreams
    Of the beautiful Annabel Lee;
And the stars never rise but I see the bright eyes
    Of the beautiful Annabel Lee;
And so, all the night-tide, I lie down by the side
Of my darling, my darling, my life and my bride,
    In her sepulchre there by the sea—
    In her tomb by the side of the sea.

❧ To Helen

Helen, thy beauty is to me,
   Like those Nicèan barks of yore
That gently, o'er a perfumed sea,
   The weary way-worn wanderer bore
   To his own native shore.

On desperate seas long wont to roam,
   Thy hyacinth hair, thy classic face,
Thy Naiad airs have brought me home
   To the glory that was Greece,
And the grandeur that was Rome.

Lo, in yon brilliant window-niche
   How statue-like I see thee stand,
   The agate lamp within thy hand,
Ah! Psyche, from the regions which
   Are holy land!

EDGAR ALLAN POE (1809–1849)

✎ A Farewell to False Love

Farewell false love, the oracle of lies,
A mortal foe and enemy to rest:
An envious boy, from whom all cares arise,
A bastard vile, a beast with rage possessed:
A way of error, a temple full of treason,
In all effects, contrary unto reason.

A poisoned serpent covered all with flowers,
Mother of sighs, and murderer of repose,
A sea of sorrows from whence are drawn
    such showers
As moisture lend to every grief that grows,
A school of guile, a net of deep deceit,
A gilded hook, that holds a poisoned bait.

A fortress foiled, which reason did defend,
A Siren song, a fever of the mind,
A maze wherein affection finds no end,
A ranging cloud that runs before the wind,
A substance like the shadow of the sun,
A goal of grief for which the wisest run.

A quenchless fire, a nurse of trembling fear,
A path that leads to peril and mishap,

stanza continues

A true retreat of sorrow and despair,
An idle boy that sleeps in pleasure's lap,
A deep mistrust of that which certain seems,
A hope of that which reason doubtful deems.

Sith then thy trains my younger years betrayed
And for my faith ingratitude I find.
And sith repentance hath my wrongs bewrayed
Whose course was ever contrary to kind.
False Love; Desire; and Beauty frail adieu
Dead is the root whence all these fancies grew.

Her Reply

If all the world and love were young,
And truth in every shepherd's tongue,
These pretty pleasures might me move
To live with thee and be thy Love.

But Time drives flocks from field to fold;
When rivers rage and rocks grow cold;
And Philomel becometh dumb;
The rest complains of cares to come.

The flowers do fade, and wanton fields
To wayward Winter reckoning yields:
A honey tongue, a heart of gall,
Is fancy's spring, but sorrow's fall.

Thy gowns, thy shoes, thy beds of roses,
Thy cap, thy kirtle, and thy posies,
Soon break, soon wither—soon forgotten,
In folly ripe, in reason rotten.

Thy belt of straw and ivy-buds,
Thy coral clasps and amber studs,—
All these in me no means can move
To come to thee and be thy Love.

But could youth last, and love still breed,
Had joys no date, nor age no need,
Then these delights my mind might move
To live with thee and be thy Love.

*(Note: This poem is a response to Christopher Marlowe's
"The Passionate Shepherd to His Love.")*

❧ Walsinghame

As you came from the holy land
   of Walsinghame
Met you not with my true love
    By the way as you came?

How shall I know your true love
    That have met many one
As I went to the holy land
    That have come, that have gone?

She is neither white nor brown
    But as the heavens fair
There is none hath a form so divine
    In the earth or the air.

Such an one did I meet, good Sir,
    Such an Angelic face,
Who like a queen, like a nymph, did appear
    By her gait, by her grace.

She hath left me here all alone,
    All alone as unknown,
Who sometimes did me lead with her self,
    And me loved as her own.

What's the cause that she leaves you alone
    And a new way doth take;
Who loved you once as her own
    And her joy did you make?

I have loved her all my youth,
    But now old, as you see,
Love likes not the falling fruit
    From the withered tree.

Know that love is a careless child
    And forgets promise past,
He is blind, he is deaf when he list
    And in faith never fast.

His desire is a dureless content
    And a trustless joy
He is won with a world of despair
    And is lost with a toy.

Of womenkind such indeed is the love
    Or the word Love abused
Under which many childish desires
    And conceits are excused.

But true Love is a durable fire
    In the mind ever burning;
Never sick, never old, never dead,
    From itself never turning.

Phyllis

Poor credulous and simple maid!
By what strange wiles art thou betrayed!
A treasure thou hast lost today
For which thou can'st no ransom pay.
How black art thou transformed with sin!
How strange a guilt gnaws me within!
Grief will convert this red to pale;
When every wake, and witsund-ale
Shall talk my shame; break, break sad heart
There is no medicine for my smart,
  No herb nor balm can cure my sorrow,
  Unless you meet again tomorrow.

❧ The Milkmaid's Epithalamium

Joy to the bridegroom and the bride
That lie by one another's side!
O fie upon the virgin beds,
No loss is gain but maidenheads.
Love quickly send the time may be
When I shall deal my rosemary!

I long to simper at a feast,
To dance, and kiss, and do the rest.
When I shall wed, and bedded be
O then the qualm comes over me,
And tells the sweetness of a theme
That I ne'er knew but in a dream.

You ladies have the blessed nights,
I pine in hope of such delights.
And silly damsel only can
Milk the cows' teats and think on man:
And sigh and wish to taste and prove
The wholesome sillabub of love.

Make haste, at once twin-brothers bear;
And leave new matter for a star.

stanza continues

THOMAS RANDOLPH (1605–1635)   173

Women and ships are never shown
So fair as when their sails be blown.
Then when the midwife hears your moan,
I'll sigh for grief that I have none.

And you, dear knight, whose every kiss
Reaps the full crop of Cupid's bliss,
Now you have found, confess and tell
That single sheets do make up hell.
And then so charitable be
To get a man to pity me.

A Birthday

My heart is like a singing bird
   Whose nest is in a watered shoot;
My heart is like an apple-tree
   Whose boughs are bent with thick-set fruit;
My heart is like a rainbow shell
   That paddles in a halcyon sea;
My heart is gladder than all these
   Because my love is come to me.

Raise me a dais of silk and down;
   Hang it with vair and purple dyes;
Carve it in doves, and pomegranates,
   And peacocks with a hundred eyes;
Work it in gold and silver grapes,
   In leaves and silver fleurs-de-lys;
Because the birthday of my life
   Is come, my love is come to me.

❧ An Apple-Gathering

I plucked pink blossoms from mine apple tree
   And wore them all that evening in my hair:
Then in due season when I went to see
   I found no apples there.

With dangling basket all along the grass
   As I had come I went the selfsame track:
My neighbours mocked me while they saw me pass
   So empty-handed back.

Lilian and Lilias smiled in trudging by,
   Their heaped-up basket teazed me like a jeer;
Sweet-voiced they sang beneath the sunset sky,
   Their mother's home was near.

Plump Gertrude passed me with her basket full,
   A stronger hand than hers helped it along;
A voice talked with her thro' the shadows cool
   More sweet to me than song.

Ah Willie, Willie, was my love less worth
   Than apples with their green leaves piled above?
I counted rosiest apples on the earth
   Of far less worth than love.

So once it was with me you stooped to talk
    Laughing and listening in this very lane:
To think that by this way we used to walk
    We shall not walk again!

I let my neighbours pass me, ones and twos
    And groups; the latest said the night grew chill,
And hastened: but I loitered, while the dews
    Fell fast I loitered still.

❧ I Loved You First

I loved you first: but afterwards your love
   Outsoaring mine, sang such a loftier song
As drowned the friendly cooings of my dove.
   Which owes the other most? my love was long,
   And yours one moment seemed to wax more
     strong;
I loved and guessed at you, you construed me
And loved me for what might or might not be—
   Nay, weights and measures do us both a wrong.
For verily love knows not 'mine' or 'thine;'
   With separate 'I' and 'thou' free love has done,
   For one is both and both are one in love:
Rich love knows nought of 'thine that is not mine;'
   Both have the strength and both the length
     thereof,
   Both of us, of the love which makes us one.

❧ Mirage

The hope I dreamed of was a dream,
    Was but a dream; and now I wake,
Exceeding comfortless, and worn, and old,
    For a dream's sake.

I hang my harp upon a tree,
    A weeping willow in a lake;
I hang my silenced harp there, wrung and snapt
    For a dream's sake.

Lie still, lie still, my breaking heart;
    My silent heart, lie still and break:
Life, and the world, and mine own self, are changed
    For a dream's sake.

❧ Promises Like Piecrust

Promise me no promises,
    So will I not promise you;
Keep we both our liberties,
    Never false and never true:
Let us hold the die uncast,
    Free to come as free to go;
For I cannot know your past,
    And of mine what can you know?

You, so warm, may once have been
    Warmer towards another one;
I, so cold, may once have seen
    Sunlight, once have felt the sun:
Who shall show us if it was
    Thus indeed in time of old?
Fades the image from the glass
    And the fortune is not told.

If you promised, you might grieve
    For lost liberty again;
If I promised, I believe
    I should fret to break the chain:
Let us be the friends we were,
    Nothing more but nothing less;
Many thrive on frugal fare
    Who would perish of excess.

CHRISTINA ROSSETTI (1830–1894)

❧ Remember

Remember me when I am gone away,
   Gone far away into the silent land;
   When you can no more hold me by the hand,
Nor I half turn to go, yet turning stay.
Remember me when no more day by day
   You tell me of our future that you planned:
   Only remember me; you understand
It will be late to counsel then or pray.
Yet if you should forget me for a while
   And afterwards remember, do not grieve:
   For if the darkness and corruption leave
   A vestige of the thoughts that once I had,
Better by far you should forget and smile
   Than that you should remember and be sad.

When I Am Dead, My Dearest

When I am dead, my dearest,
Sing no sad songs for me;
Plant thou no roses at my head,
Nor shady cypress-tree:
Be the green grass above me
With showers and dewdrops wet;
And if thou wilt, remember,
And if thou wilt, forget.

I shall not see the shadows,
I shall not feel the rain;
I shall not hear the nightingale
Sing on, as if in pain:
And dreaming through the twilight
That doth not rise nor set,
Haply I may remember,
And haply may forget.

CHRISTINA ROSSETTI (1830–1894)

"Two separate divided silences,"

Two separate divided silences,
　　Which, brought together, would find loving
　　　　voice;
　　Two glances which together would rejoice
In love, now lost like starts beyond dark trees;
Two hands apart whose touch alone gives ease;
　　Two bosoms which, heart-shrined with mutual
　　　　flame,
　　Would, meeting in one clasp, be made the same;
Two souls, the shores wave mocked of sundering
　　seas:—

Such are we now. Ah! may our hope forecast
　　Indeed one hour again, when on this stream
　　Of darkened love once more the light shall
　　　　gleam?—
An hour how slow to come, how quickly past,—
Which blooms and fades, and only leaves at last,
　　Faint as shed flowers, the attenuated dream.

❧ One Girl

I

Like the sweet apple which reddens upon the
  topmost bough,
Atop on the topmost twig,—which the pluckers
  forgot, somehow,—
Forgot it not, nay; but got it not, for none could
  get it till now.

II

Like the wild hyacinth flower which on the hills
  is found,
Which the passing feet of the shepherds for ever
  tear and wound,
Until the purple blossom is trodden in the ground.

Translated from the Greek by
Dante Gabriel Rossetti (1828–1882)

SAPPHO (7TH CENTURY B.C.)

❧ On the Happy Corydon and Phyllis

Young Corydon and Phyllis
  Sat in a lovely grove,
Contriving crowns of lilies,
  Repeating toys of love,
And something else, but what I dare not name.

But as they were a-playing,
  She ogled so the swain;
It saved her plainly saying
  Let's kiss to ease our pain:
And something else, but what I dare not name.

A thousand times he kissed her,
  Laying her on the green;
But as he farther pressed her,
  A pretty leg was seen:
And something else, but what I dare not name.

So many beauties viewing,
  His ardour still increased;
And greater joys pursuing,
  He wandered o'er her breast:
And something else, but what I dare not name.

A last effort she trying,
  His passion to withstand;

stanza continues

SIR CHARLES SEDLEY (1639?–1701)   185

Cried, but it was faintly crying,
    Pray take away your hand:
And something else, but what I dare not name.

Young Corydon grown bolder,
    The minutes would improve;
This is the time, he told her,
    To show you how I love;
And something else, but what I dare not name.

The nymph seemed almost dying,
    Dissolved in amorous heat;
She kissed and told him sighing,
    My dear your love is great:
And something else, but what I dare not name.

But Phyllis did recover
    Much sooner than the swain;
She blushing asked her lover,
    Shall we not kiss again:
And something else, but what I dare not name.

Thus Love his revels keeping,
    'Til Nature at a stand;
From talk they fell to sleeping,
    Holding each other's hand;
And something else, but what I dare not name.

❧ To Cloris

Cloris, I cannot say your eyes
Did my unwary heart surprise;
Nor will I swear it was your face,
Your shape, or any nameless grace:
For you are so entirely fair,
To love a part, injustice were;
No drowning man can know which drop
Of water his last breath did stop;
So when the stars in heaven appear,
And join to make the night look clear;
The light we no one's bounty call,
But the obliging gift of all.
He that does lips or hands adore,
Deserves them only, and no more;
But I love all, and every part,
And nothing less can ease my heart.
Cupid, that lover, weakly strikes,
Who can express what 'tis he likes.

❧ Sonnet XVIII

Shall I compare thee to a summer's day?
   Thou art more lovely and more temperate:
Rough winds do shake the darling buds of May,
   And summer's lease hath all too short a date:
Sometime too hot the eye of heaven shines,
   And often is his gold complexion dimmed;
And every fair from fair sometime declines,
   By chance, or nature's changing course
     untrimmed;
But thy eternal summer shall not fade,
   Nor lose possession of that fair thou owest,
Nor shall death brag thou wanderest in his shade,
   When in eternal lines to time thou growest;
    So long as men can breathe, or eyes can see,
    So long lives this, and this gives life to thee.

Sonnet XXIX

When in disgrace with fortune and men's eyes,
I all alone beweep my outcast state,
And trouble deaf heaven with my bootless cries,
And look upon myself, and curse my fate,
Wishing me like to one more rich in hope,
Featur'd like him, like him with friends possess'd,
Desiring this man's art, and that man's scope,
With what I most enjoy contented least;
Yet in these thoughts myself almost despising,
Haply I think on thee, and then my state,
Like to the lark at break of day arising
From sullen earth, sings hymns at heaven's gate;
 For thy sweet love rememb'red such wealth
  brings,
  That then I scorn to change my state with kings.

❧ Sonnet XXX

When to the sessions of sweet silent thought
I summon up remembrance of things past,
I sigh the lack of many a thing I sought,
And with old woes new wail my dear time's waste:
Then can I drown an eye, unus'd to flow,
For precious friends hid in death's dateless night,
And weep afresh love's long since cancell'd woe,
And moan the expense of many a vanish'd sight:
Then can I grieve at grievances foregone,
And heavily from woe to woe tell o'er
The sad account of fore-bemoan'd moan,
Which I new pay as if not paid before.
   But if the while I think on thee, dear friend,
    All losses are restor'd and sorrows end.

❧ Sonnet LVII

Being your slave, what should I do but tend
Upon the hours and times of your desire?
I have no precious time at all to spend,
Nor services to do, till you require.
Nor dare I chide the world-without-end hour
Whilst I, my sovereign, watch the clock for you,
Nor think the bitterness of absence sour
When you have bid your servant once adieu;
Nor dare I question with my jealous thought
Where you may be, or your affairs suppose,
But, like a sad slave, stay and think of nought,
Save, where you are, how happy you make those.
  So true a fool is love that in your will,
    Though you do any thing, he thinks no ill.

❧ Sonnet LXVI

Tir'd with all these, for restful death I cry,
As, to behold desert a beggar born,
And needy nothing trimm'd in jollity,
And purest faith unhappily forsworn,
And gilded honour shamefully misplac'd,
And maiden virtue rudely strumpeted,
And right perfection wrongfully disgrac'd,
And strength by limping sway disabled,
And art made tongue-tied by authority,
And folly, doctor-like, controlling skill,
And simple truth, miscall'd simplicity,
And captive good attending captain ill:
    Tir'd with all these, from these I would be gone,
    Save that, to die, I leave my love alone.

❧ Sonnet LXXIII

That time of year thou may'st in me behold
  When yellow leaves, or none, or few, do hang
Upon those boughs which shake against the cold,
  Bare ruined choirs, where late the sweet birds
    sang.
In me thou see'st the twilight of such day
  As after sunset fadeth in the west;
Which by and by black night doth take away,
  Death's second self, that seals up all in rest.
In me thou see'st the glowing of such fire,
  That on the ashes of his youth doth lie,
As the death-bed whereon it must expire,
  Consumed with that which it was nourished by.
    This thou perceiv'st, which makes thy love
      more strong,
     To love that well which thou must leave
      ere long.

Sonnet CXVI

Let me not to the marriage of true minds
Admit impediments. Love is not love
Which alters when it alteration finds,
Or bends with the remover to remove:
Oh, no! it is an ever-fixèd mark,
That looks on tempests and is never shaken;
It is the star to every wandering bark,
Whose worth's unknown, although his height
  be taken.
Love's not Time's fool, though rosy lips and cheeks
Within his bending sickle's compass come;
Love alters not with his brief hours and weeks,
But bears it out even to the edge of doom.
  If this be error and upon me proved,
    I never writ, nor no man ever loved.

Sonnet CXXIX

Th'expense of spirit in a waste of shame
Is lust in action, and till action, lust
Is perjur'd, murd'rous, bloody, full of blame,
Savage, extreme, rude, cruel, not to trust;
Enjoy'd no sooner but despised straight;
Past reason hunted, and no sooner had,
Past reason hated as a swallowed bait,
On purpose laid to make the taker mad;
Mad in pursuit and in possession so;
Had, having, and in quest, to have, extreme;
A bliss in proof, and prov'd, a very woe;
Before a joy propos'd, behind a dream,
   All this the world well knows yet none
      knows well;
    To shun the heaven that leads men to this hell.

Sonnet CXXX

My mistress' eyes are nothing like the sun;
Coral is far more red than her lips' red:
If snow be white, why then her breasts are dun;
If hairs be wires, black wires grow on her head.
I have seen roses damasked, red and white,
But no such roses see I in her cheeks;
And in some perfumes is there more delight
Than in the breath that from my mistress reeks.
I love to hear her speak; yet well I know
That music hath a far more pleasing sound:
I grant I never saw a goddess go,
My mistress, when she walks, treads on the
    ground;
  And yet, by heaven, I think my love as rare
  As any she belied with false compare.

Sonnet CXLI

In faith, I do not love thee with mine eyes,
For they in thee a thousand errors note;
But 'tis my heart that loves what they despise,
Who in despite of view is pleas'd to dote;
Nor are mine ears with thy tongue's tune
    delighted;
Nor tender feeling to base touches prone,
Nor taste, nor smell, desire to be invited
To any sensual feast with thee alone:
But my five wits nor my five senses can
Dissuade one foolish heart from serving thee,
Who leaves unsway'd the likeness of a man,
Thy proud heart's slave and vassal wretch to be:
  Only my plague thus far I count my gain,
  That she that makes me sin awards my pain.

❧ Feste's Song

from *TWELFTH NIGHT*

O mistress mine, where are you roaming?
O! stay and hear; your true love's coming,
   That can sing both high and low.
Trip no further, pretty sweeting;
Journeys end in lovers meeting,
   Every wise man's son doth know.

What is love? 'Tis not hereafter;
Present mirth hath present laughter;
   What's to come is still unsure.
In delay there lies no plenty;
Then come kiss me, sweet and twenty;
   Youth's a stuff will not endure.

ॐ "Who is Silvia? what is she,"

from *THE TWO GENTLEMEN OF VERONA*

Who is Silvia? what is she,
   That all our swains commend her?
Holy, fair, and wise is she;
   The heaven such grace did lend her,
That she might admired be.

Is she kind as she is fair, —
   For beauty lives with kindness?
Love doth to her eyes repair,
   To help him of his blindness;
And, being help'd, inhabits there.

Then to Silvia let us sing,
   That Silvia is excelling;
She excels each mortal thing
   Upon the dull earth dwelling:
To her let us garlands bring.

❧ Love's Philosophy

The fountains mingle with the river
   And the rivers with the Ocean,
The winds of Heaven mix for ever
   With a sweet emotion;
Nothing in the world is single;
   All things by a law divine
In one spirit meet and mingle.
   Why not I with thine? —

See the mountains kiss high Heaven
   And the waves clasp one another;
No sister-flower would be forgiven
   If it disdained its brother;
And the sunlight clasps the earth
   And the moonbeams kiss the sea:
What is all this sweet work worth
   If thou kiss not me?

"My true love hath my heart, and I have his,"

My true love hath my heart, and I have his,
By just exchange, one for the other given.
I hold his dear, and mine he cannot miss:
There never was a better bargain driven.
His heart in me, keeps me and him in one,
My heart in him, his thoughts and senses guides:
He loves my heart, for once it was his own:
I cherish his, because in me it bides.
His heart his wound receivèd from my sight:
My heart was wounded with his wounded heart,
For as from me, on him his hurt did light,
So still methought in me his hurt did smart:
   Both equal hurt, in this change sought our bliss:
    My true love hath my heart and I have his.

"With how sad steps, O moon, thou climb'st the skies!"

With how sad steps, O moon, thou climb'st the
    skies!
How silently, and with how wan a face!
What! may it be that even in heavenly place
That busy archer his sharp arrow tries?
Sure, if that long-with-love-acquainted eyes
Can judge of love, thou feel'st a lover's case:
I read it in thy looks; thy languished grace
To me, that feel the like, thy state descries.
Then, even of fellowship, O Moon, tell me,
Is constant love deemed there but want of wit?
Are beauties there as proud as here they be?
Do they above love to be loved, and yet
    Those lovers scorn whom that love doth possess?
    Do they call 'virtue' there—ungratefulness?

The Author Apologizes to a Lady for His Being a Little Man

Yes, contumelious fair, you scorn
The amorous dwarf that courts you to his arms,
But ere you leave him quite forlorn,
And to some youth 'gigantic' yield your
charms,
Hear him—oh hear him, if you will not try,
And let your judgement check th' ambition of
your eye.

Say, is it carnage makes the man?
Is to be monstrous really to be great?
Say, is it wise or just to scan
Your lover's worth by quantity or weight?
Ask your mamma and nurse, if it be so;
Nurse and mamma I ween shall jointly answer, no.

The less the body to the view,
The soul (like springs in closer durance pent)
Is all exertion, ever new,
Unceasing, unextinguished, and unspent;
Still pouring forth executive desire,
As bright, as brisk, and lasting, as the vestal fire.

continues

Does thy young bosom pant for fame;
Would'st thou be of posterity the toast?
    The poets shall ensure thy name,
Who magnitude of *mind* not *body* boast.
Laurels on bulky bards as rarely grow,
As on the sturdy oak the virtuous mistletoe.

    Look in the glass, survey that cheek —
Where Flora has with all her roses blushed;
    The shape so tender, — look so meek —
The breasts made to be pressed, not to be
            crushed —
Then turn to me, — turn with obliging eyes,
Nor longer nature's works, in miniature, despise.

    Young Ammon did the world subdue,
Yet had not more external man than I;
    Ah! charmer, should I conquer you,
With him in fame, as well as size, I'll vie.
Then, scornful nymph, come forth to yonder
            grove,
Where I defy, and challenge, all thy utmost love.

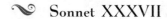

Sonnet XXXVII

from *AMORETTI*

What guyle is this, that those her golden tresses,
She doth attyre under a net of gold:
And with sly skill so cunningly them dresses,
That which is gold or heare, may scarse be told?
Is it that mens frayle eyes, which gaze too bold,
She may entangle in that golden snare:
And being caught may craftily enfold
Theyr weaker harts, which are not wel aware?
Take heed therefore, myne eyes, how ye doe stare
Henceforth too rashly on that guilefull net,
In which if ever ye entrapped are,
Out of her bands ye by no meanes shall get.
Fondnesse it were for any being free,
To covet fetters, though they golden bee.

❧ Sonnet LXXV

from *AMORETTI*

One day I wrote her name upon the strand,
   But came the waves and washed it away:
Again I wrote it with a second hand,
   But came the tide, and made my pains his prey.
'Vain man,' said she, 'thou do'st in vain assay,
   A mortal thing so to immortalize,
For I myself shall like to this decay,
   And eek my name be wipèd out likewise.'
'Not so,' quoth I, 'let baser things devise
   To die in dust, but you shall live by fame:
My verse your virtues rare shall eternize,
   And in the heavens write your glorious name,
     Where, whenas death shall all the world subdue,
     Our love shall live, and later life renew.'

"Out upon it, I have loved"

Out upon it, I have loved
   Three whole days together;
And am like to love three more,
   If it hold fair weather.

Time shalt moult away his wings
   Ere he shall discover
In the whole wide world again
   Such a constant lover.

But a pox upon't, no praise
   There is due at all to me:
Love with me had made no stays,
   Had it any been but she.

Had it any been but she
   And that very very face,
There had been at least ere this
   A dozen dozen in her place.

⌽ "Why so pale and wan, fond lover?"

Why so pale and wan, fond lover?
  Prithee, why so pale?
Will, when looking well can't move her,
  Looking ill prevail?
  Prithee, why so pale?

Why so dull and mute, young sinner?
  Prithee, why so mute?
Will, when speaking well can't win her,
  Saying nothing do 't?
  Prithee, why so mute?

Quit, quit for shame! This will not move;
  This cannot take her.
If of herself she will not love,
  Nothing can make her:
  The devil take her.

Love and Sleep

Lying asleep between the strokes of night
   I saw my love lean over my sad bed,
   Pale as the duskiest lily's leaf or head,
Smooth-skinned and dark, with the bare throat
     made to bite,
Too wan for blushing and too warm for white,
   But perfect-coloured without white or red.
   And her lips opened amorously, and said—
I wist not what, saving one word—Delight.

And all her face was honey to my mouth,
   And all her body pasture to mine eyes;
    The long lithe arms and hotter hands than fire,
The quivering flanks, hair smelling of the south,
   The bright light feet, the splendid supple thighs
    And glittering eyelids of my soul's desire.

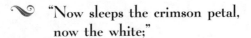

"Now sleeps the crimson petal, now the white;"

from *THE PRINCESS*

Now sleeps the crimson petal, now the white;
Nor waves the cypress in the palace walk;
Nor winks the gold fin in the porphyry font:
The fire-fly wakens: waken thou with me.

Now droops the milkwhite peacock like a ghost,
And like a ghost she glimmers on to me.

Now lies the Earth all Danaë to the stars,
And all thy heart lies open unto me.

Now slides the silent meteor on, and leaves
A shining furrow, as thy thoughts in me.

Now folds the lily all her sweetness up,
And slips into the bosom of the lake:
So fold thyself, my dearest, thou, and slip
Into my bosom and be lost in me.

❧ In My Craft or Sullen Art

In my craft or sullen art
Exercised in the still night
When only the moon rages
And the lovers lie abed
With all their griefs in their arms,
I labour by singing light
Not for ambition or bread
Or the strut and trade of charms
On the ivory stages
But for the common wages
Of their most secret heart.

Not for the proud man apart
From the raging moon I write
On these spindrift pages
Nor for the towering dead
With their nightingales and psalms
But for the lovers, their arms
Round the griefs of the ages,
Who pay no praise or wages
Nor heed my craft or art.

❧ And You, Helen

And you, Helen, what should I give you?
So many things I would give you
Had I an infinite great store
Offered me and I stood before
To choose. I would give you youth,
All kinds of loveliness and truth.
A clear eye as good as mine,
Lands, waters, flowers, wine,
As many children as your heart
Might wish for, a far better art
Than mine can be, all you have lost
Upon the travelling waters tossed,
Or given to me. If I could choose
Freely in that great treasure-house
Anything from any shelf,
I would give you back yourself,
And power to discriminate
What you want and want it not too late,
Many fair days free from care
And heart to enjoy both foul and fair,
And myself, too, if I could find
Where it lay hidden and it proved kind.

❧ An Arab Love-Song

The hunched camels of the night
Trouble the bright
And silver waters of the moon.
The Maiden of the Morn will soon
Through Heaven stray and sing,
Star-gathering.

Now while the dark about our loves is strewn,
Light of my dark, blood of my heart, O come!
And night will catch her breath up, and be dumb.

Leave thy father, leave thy mother
And thy brother;
Leave the black tents of thy tribe apart!
Am I not thy father and thy brother,
And thy mother?
And thou—what needest with thy tribe's black tents
Who hast the red pavillion of my heart?

FRANCIS THOMPSON (1859–1907)

❧ Song

Go, lovely rose!
Tell her that wastes her time and me
    That now she knows,
When I resemble her to thee,
How sweet and fair she seems to be.

Tell her that's young,
And shuns to have her graces spied,
    That hadst thou sprung
In deserts, where no men abide,
Thou must have uncommended died.

Small is the worth
Of beauty from the light retired;
    Bid her come forth,
Suffer herself to be desired,
And not blush so to be admired.

Then die! that she
The common fate of all things rare
    May read in thee;
How small a part of time they share
That are so wondrous sweet and fair!

From Pent-Up Aching Rivers

From pent-up aching rivers,
From that of myself without which I were nothing,
From what I am determin'd to make illustrious,
    even if I stand sole among men,
From my own voice resonant, singing the phallus,
Singing the song of procreation,
Singing the need of superb children and therein
    superb grown people,
Singing the muscular urge and the blending,
Singing the bedfellow's song, (O resistless yearning!
O for any and each the body correlative attracting!
O for you whoever you are your correlative body!
    O it, more than all else, you delighting!)
From the hungry gnaw that eats me night and day,
From native moments, from bashful pains, singing
    them,
Seeking something yet unfound though I have
    diligently sought it many a long year,
Singing the true song of the soul fitful at random,
Renascent with grossest Nature or among animals,
Of that, of them and what goes with them my
    poems informing,
Of the smell of apples and lemons, of the pairing
    of birds,

continues

Of the wet of woods, of the lapping of waves,
Of the mad pushes of waves upon the land, I them
    chanting,
The overture lightly sounding, the strain anticipating,
The welcome nearness, the sight of the perfect body,
The swimmer swimming naked in the bath, or
    motionless on his back lying and floating,
The female form approaching, I pensive, love-flesh
    tremulous aching,
The divine list for myself or you or for any one
    making,
The face, the limbs, the index from head to foot,
    and what it arouses,
The mystic deliria, the madness amorous, the utter
    abandonment,
(Hark close and still what I now whisper to you,
I love you, O you entirely possess me,
O that you and I escape from the rest and go
    utterly off, free and lawless,
Two hawks in the air, two fishes swimming in the
    sea not more lawless than we;)
The furious storm through me careering, I
    passionately trembling,
The oath of the inseparableness of two together, of
    the woman that loves me and whom I love more
    than my life, that oath swearing,
(O I willingly stake all for you,
O let me be lost if it must be so!

O you and I! what is it to us what the rest do or
    think?
What is all else to us? only that we enjoy each
    other and exhaust each other if it must be so;)
From the master, the pilot I yield the vessel to,
The general commanding me, commanding all,
    from him permission taking,
From time the programme hastening, (I have
    loiter'd too long as it is,)
From sex, from the warp and from the woof,
From privacy, from frequent repinings alone,
From plenty of persons near and yet the right person
    not near,
From the soft sliding of hands over me and
    thrusting of fingers through my hair and beard,
From the long sustain'd kiss upon the mouth or
    bosom,
From the close pressure that makes me or any man
    drunk, fainting with excess,
From what the divine husband knows, from the
    work of fatherhood,
From exultation, victory and relief from the
    bedfellow's embrace in the night,
From the act-poems of eyes, hands, hips and bosoms,
From the cling of the trembling arm,
From the bending curve and the clinch,

continues

From side by side the pliant coverlet off-throwing,
From the one so unwilling to have me leave, and
   me just as unwilling to leave,
(Yet a moment O tender waiter, and I return,)
From the hour of shining stars and dropping dews,
From the night a moment I emerging flitting out,
Celebrate you act divine and you children
   prepared for,
And you stalwart loins.

❧ *from* I Sing the Body Electric

1

I sing the body electric,
The armies of those I love engirth me and I engirth
   them,
They will not let me off till I go with them, respond
   to them,
And discorrupt them, and charge them full with the
   charge of the soul.

Was it doubted that those who corrupt their own
   bodies conceal themselves?
And if those who defile the living are as bad as they
   who defile the dead?
And if the body does not do fully as much as
   the soul?
And if the body were not the soul, what is the soul?

2

The love of the body of man or woman balks
   account, the body itself balks account,
That of the male is perfect, and that of the female
   is perfect.

continues

WALT WHITMAN (1819–1892)

The expression of the face balks account,
But the expression of a well-made man appears not
only in his face,
It is in his limbs and joints also, it is curiously in
the joints of his hips and wrists,
It is in his walk, the carriage of his neck, the flex
of his waist and knees, dress does not hide him,
The strong sweet quality he has strikes through the
cotton and broadcloth,
To see him pass conveys as much as the best poem,
perhaps more,
You linger to see his back, and the back of his neck
and shoulder-side.

The sprawl and fulness of babes, the bosoms and
heads of women, the folds of their dress, their
style as we pass in the street, the contour of their
shape downwards,
The swimmer naked in the swimming-bath, seen as
he swims through the transparent green-shine,
or lies with his face up and rolls silently to and
fro in the heave of the water,
The bending forward and backward of rowers in
row-boats, the horseman in his saddle,
Girls, mothers, house-keepers, in all their
performances,

stanza continues

The group of laborers seated at noon-time with
their open dinner kettles, and their wives waiting,
The female soothing a child, the farmer's daughter
in the garden or cow-yard,
The young fellow hoeing corn, the sleigh-driver
driving his six horses through the crowd,
The wrestle of wrestlers, two apprentice-boys, quite
grown, lusty, good-natured, native-born, out on
the vacant lot at sundown after work,
The coats and caps thrown down, the embrace of
love and resistance,
The upper-hold and under-hold, the hair rumpled
over and blinding the eyes;
The march of firemen in their own costumes, the
play of masculine muscle through clean-setting
trowsers and waist-straps,
The slow return from the fire, the pause when the
bell strikes suddenly again, and the listening on
the alert,
The natural, perfect, varied attitudes, the bent
head, the curv'd neck and the counting;
Such-like I love—I loosen myself, pass freely, am
at the mother's breast with the little child,
Swim with the swimmers, wrestle with wrestlers,
march in line with the firemen, and pause, listen,
count.

continues

WALT WHITMAN (1819–1892)   221

3

I knew a man, a common farmer, the father of five
  sons,
And in them the fathers of sons, and in them the
  fathers of sons.
This man was of wonderful vigor, calmness, beauty
  of person,
The shape of his head, the pale yellow and white of
  his hair and beard, the immeasurable meaning of
  his black eyes, the richness and breadth of his
  manners,
These I used to go and visit him to see, he was
  wise also,
He was six feet tall, he was over eighty years old,
  his sons were massive, clean, bearded, tan-faced,
  handsome,
They and his daughters loved him, all who saw
  him loved him,
They did not love him by allowance, they loved
  him with personal love,
He drank water only, the blood show'd like scarlet
  through the clear-brown skin of his face,
He was a frequent gunner and fisher, he sail'd his
  boat himself, he had a fine one presented to him
  by a ship-joiner, he had fowling-pieces presented
  to him by men that loved him,

When he went with his five sons and many grand-
 sons to hunt or fish, you would pick him out as
 the most beautiful and vigorous of the gang,
You would wish long and long to be with him, you
 would wish to sit by him in the boat that you
 and he might touch each other.

4

I have perceiv'd that to be with those I like is
 enough,
To stop in company with the rest at evening is
 enough,
To be surrounded by beautiful, curious, breathing,
 laughing flesh is enough,
To pass among them or touch any one, or rest my
 arm ever so lightly round his or her neck for a
 moment, what is this then?
I do not ask any more delight, I swim in it as in
 a sea.

There is something in staying close to men and
 women and looking on them, and in the contact
 and odor of them, that pleases the soul well,
All things please the soul, but these please the
 soul well.

❧ "When I heard at the close of the day"

from *CALAMUS*

When I heard at the close of the day how my name
    had been receiv'd with plaudits in the capitol,
    still it was not a happy night for me that
    follow'd,
And else when I carous'd, or when my plans were
    accomplish'd, still I was not happy,
But the day when I rose at dawn from the bed of
    perfect health, refresh'd, singing, inhaling the
    ripe breath of autumn,
When I saw the full moon in the west grow pale
    and disappear in the morning light,
When I wander'd alone over the beach, and
    undressing bathed, laughing with the cool
    waters, and saw the sun rise,
And when I thought how my dear friend my lover
    was on his way coming, O then I was happy,
O then each breath tasted sweeter, and all that day
    my food nourish'd me more, and the beautiful
    day pass'd well,
And the next came with equal joy, and with the
    next at evening came my friend,
And that night while all was still I heard the waters
    roll slowly continually up the shores,

I heard the hissing rustle of the liquid and sands as
    directed to me whispering to congratulate me,
For the one I love most lay sleeping by me under
    the same cover in the cool night,
In the stillness in the autumn moonbeams his face
    was inclined toward me,
And his arm lay lightly around my breast—and
    that night I was happy.

Love Song

Sweep the house clean,
hang fresh curtains
in the windows
put on a new dress
and come with me!
The elm is scattering
its little loaves
of sweet smells
from a white sky!

Who shall hear of us
in the time to come?
Let him say there was
a burst of fragrance
from black branches.

The Widow's Lament in Springtime

Sorrow is my own yard
where the new grass
flames as it has flamed
often before but not
with the cold fire
that closes round me this year.
Thirtyfive years
I lived with my husband.
The plumtree is white today
with masses of flowers.
Masses of flowers
load the cherry branches
and color some bushes
yellow and some red
but the grief in my heart
is stronger than they
for though they were my joy
formerly, today I notice them
and turn away forgetting.
Today my son told me
that in the meadows,
at the edge of the heavy woods
in the distance, he saw
trees of white flowers.

continues

I feel that I would like
to go there
and fall into those flowers
and sink into the marsh near them.

❧ Love and Life

All my past life is mine no more;
  The flying hours are gone,
Like transitory dreams given o'er
Whose images are kept in store
  By memory alone.

Whatever is to come is not:
  How can it then be mine?
The present moment's all my lot,
And that, as fast as it is got,
  Phyllis, is wholly thine.

Then talk not of inconstancy,
  False hearts, and broken vows;
If I, by miracle, can be
This livelong minute true to thee,
  'Tis all that heaven allows.

❧ She Was a Phantom of Delight

She was a Phantom of delight
When first she gleamed upon my sight;
A lovely Apparition, sent
To be a moment's ornament;
Her eyes as stars of Twilight fair;
Like Twilight's, too, her dusky hair;
But all things else about her drawn
From May-time and the cheerful Dawn;
A dancing Shape, an Image gay,
To haunt, to startle, and way-lay.

I saw her upon nearer view,
A Spirit, yet a Woman too!
Her household motions light and free,
And steps of virgin-liberty;
A countenance in which did meet
Sweet records, promises as sweet;
A Creature not too bright or good
For human nature's daily food;
For transient sorrows, simple wiles,
Praise, blame, love, kisses, tears, and smiles.

And now I see with eye serene
The very pulse of the machine;

stanza continues

A Being breathing thoughtful breath,
A Traveler between life and death;
The reason firm, the temperate will,
Endurance, foresight, strength, and skill;
A perfect Woman, nobly planned,
To warn, to comfort, and command;
And yet a Spirit still, and bright
With something of angelic light.

Surprised by Joy

Surprised by joy—impatient as the Wind
I turned to share the transport—Oh! with whom
But thee, deep buried in the silent tomb,
That spot which no vicissitude can find?
Love, faithful love, recalled thee to my mind—
But how could I forget thee? Through what power,
Even for the least division of an hour,
Have I been so beguiled as to be blind
To my most grievous loss!—That thought's return
Was the worst pang that sorrow ever bore,
Save one, one only, when I stood forlorn,
Knowing my heart's best treasure was no more;
That neither present time, nor years unborn
Could to my sight that heavenly face restore.

Song

from *URANIA*

Love what art thou? A vain thought
  In our minds by phant'sie wrought,
  Idle smiles did thee beget
  While fond wishes made the net
  Which so many fools have caught;

Love what art thou? light, and fair,
  Fresh as morning, clear as th'air,
  But too soon thy evening change
  Makes thy worth with coldness range;
  Still thy joy is mixed with care.

Love what art thou? A sweet flow'r
  Once full blown, dead in an hour,
  Dust in wind as staid remains
  As thy pleasure, or our gains
  If thy humor change to lour.

Love what art thou? childish, vain,
  Firm as bubbles made by rain;
  Wantonness thy greatest pride,
  These foul faults thy virtues hide,
  But babes can no staidness gain.

LADY MARY WROTH (1586–1640)   233

Love what art thou? causeless curse,
   Yet alas these not the worst,
   Much more of thee may be said
   But thy law I once obeyed
   Therefore say no more at first.

"Is to leave all and take the thread of Love,"

Is to leave all and take the thread of Love,
Which line straight leads unto the soul's content,
Where choice delights with pleasure's wings do
    move,
An idle fant'sy never room had lent.
When chaste thoughts guide us, then our minds
    are bent
To take that good which ills from us remove:
Light of true love brings fruit which none repent;
But constant lovers seek and wish to prove.
Love is the shining star of blessings light,
The fervent fire of zeal, the root of peace,
The lasting lamp, fed with the oil of right,
Image of faith, and womb for joys increase.
Love is true virtue, and his ends delight,
His flames are joys, his bands true lovers might.

"Alas! madam, for stealing of a kiss,"

Alas! madam, for stealing of a kiss,
    Have I so much your mind then offended?
Have I then done so grievously amiss,
    That by no means it may be amended?
Then revenge you, and the next way is this:
    Another kiss shall have my life ended.
For to my mouth the first my heart did suck,
The next shall clean out of my breast it pluck.

"I abide and abide and better abide"

I abide and abide and better abide
(And after the old proverb) the happy day;
And ever my lady to me doth say
'Let me alone and I will provide'.
I abide and abide and tarry the tide,
And with abiding speed well ye may!
Thus do I abide I wot alway
Not her obtaining nor yet denied.
Aye me! this long abiding
Seemeth to me as who sayeth
A prolonging of a dying death
Or a refusing of a desired thing.
Much were it better for me to be plain
Than to say 'abide' and yet not obtain.

❧ The Lover Rejoiceth

Tangled was I in Love's snare,
Oppressed with pain, torment with care;
Of grief right sure, of joy full bare,
Clean in despair by cruelty.
But ha! ha! ha! full well is me,
For I am now at liberty.

The woeful days so full of pain,
The weary nights all spent in vain,
The labor lost for no small gain,
To write them all it will not be.
But ha! ha! ha! full well is me,
For I am now at liberty.

With feignèd words which were but wind,
To long delays was I assign'd;
Her wily looks my wits did blind;
Whate'er she would I would agree.
But ha! ha! ha! full well is me,
For I am now at liberty.

Was never bird tangled in lime,
That broke away in better time,
Than I, that rotten boughs did climb,

stanza continuese

And had no hurt but 'scapèd free.
Now ha! ha! ha! full well is me,
For I am now at liberty.

They Flee from Me

They flee from me that sometime did me seek
  With naked foot stalking in my chamber.
I have seen them gentle tame and meek
  That now are wild and do not remember
  That sometime they put themselves in danger
To take bread at my hand; and now they range
Busily seeking with a continual change.

Thanked be fortune, it hath been otherwise
  Twenty times better; but once in special,
In thin array after a pleasant guise,
  When her loose gown from her shoulders
    did fall,
  And she me caught in her arms long and small;
And therewithal sweetly did me kiss,
And softly said, *Dear heart, how like you this?*

It was no dream, I lay broad waking.
  But all is turned thorough my gentleness
Into a strange fashion of forsaking;
  And I have leave to go of her goodness
  And she also to use newfangleness.
But since that I so kindly am served,
I would fain know what she hath deserved.

❧ Down by the Salley Gardens

Down by the salley gardens my love and I
  did meet;
She passed the salley gardens with little snow-
  white feet.
She bid me take love easy, as the leaves grow on
  the tree;
But I, being young and foolish, with her would
  not agree.

In a field by the river my love and I did stand,
And on my leaning shoulder she laid her snow-
  white hand.
She bid me take life easy, as the grass grows on
  the weirs;
But I was young and foolish, and now am full
  of tears.

To an Isle in the Water

Shy one, shy one,
Shy one of my heart,
She moves in the firelight
Pensively apart.

She carries in the dishes,
And lays them in a row.
To an isle in the water
With her would I go.

She carries in the candles,
And lights the curtained room,
Shy in the doorway
And shy in the gloom;

And shy as a rabbit,
Helpful and shy.
To an isle in the water
With her would I fly.

❧ When You Are Old

When you are old and gray and full of sleep,
And nodding by the fire, take down this book,
And slowly read, and dream of the soft look
Your eyes had once, and of their shadows deep;

How many loved your moments of glad grace,
And loved your beauty with love false or true;
But one man loved the pilgrim soul in you,
And loved the sorrows of your changing face.

And bending down beside the glowing bars
Murmur, a little sadly, how love fled
And paced upon the mountains overhead
And hid his face amid a crowd of stars.

Index of First Lines

INDEX OF FIRST LINES   247

Acknowledgments